How to Invest in
Bonds

How to Invest in

Bonds

Revised and Updated

Hugh C. Sherwood

McGraw-Hill Book Company

New York St. Louis San Francisco Bogotá Guatemala
Hamburg Lisbon Madrid Mexico Montreal
Panama Paris San Juan São Paulo Tokyo Toronto

Reprinted by arrangement with Walker and Company
First McGraw-Hill paperback edition, 1983

1 2 3 4 5 6 7 8 9 FGRFGR 8 7 6 5 4 3

ISBN 0-07-056684-4

Library of Congress Cataloging in Publication Data

Sherwood, Hugh C.
  How to invest in bonds.

  Originally published: New York: Walker, ©1983.
  Includes index.
  1. Bonds.   I. Title.
HG4651.S47   1983b   332.63'23   83-9863
ISBN 0-07-056684-4

Contents

Preface

This book is not written for the professional bond analyst, dealer or trader. Rather it is written for both the average investor and the novice. It seeks to provide these investors with a basic working knowledge of different kinds of bonds, bond funds and bond markets.

You will not learn how to make a million dollars in twelve easy lessons. Life is rarely that simple. And even if it were, I do not believe in formulas that promise easy success in an uncertain world. If the book increases its readers' knowledge of bonds and helps them conserve their financial resources, obtain a good income from them and possibly increase their size, it will have served its purpose.

In writing this book I have been indebted to many people for providing me with information and counsel. They include, alphabetically in accordance with their corporate affiliations: Kevin Carroll, a partner of Gintel & Co.; James Lebenthal, chairman of Lebenthal & Co.; Preston Harrington III, an analyst with Merrill Lynch, Pierce, Fenner & Smith; Frank P. Wendt, chairman of

John Nuveen & Co.; Douglas McAllister, a vice president of Prudential-Bache Securities; Alan W. Leeds, a partner of L. F. Rothschild, Unterberg, Towbin; Samuel Thorne, a senior vice president of Scudder, Stevens & Clark; Jon Martin Zayachek, a second vice president of Smith Barney, Harris Upham; Thomas G. Fendrich, Hyman Grossman, Richard E. Huff and Roy Weinberger, all vice presidents of Standard & Poor's; and Douglas Harrell, a vice president of Van Kampen Merritt.

I have enjoyed writing this book, as I did its earlier edition, and have learned a great deal in the process. I hope you will be similarly served.

—*Hugh C. Sherwood*
White Plains, New York

Introduction: The World of Bonds

The world of bonds has changed markedly in the past decade. What was once a quiet, staid sphere in comparison with the worlds of stocks and commodities has become unsettled, even turbulent. No end is in sight.

What exactly has changed? And why?

Interest rates on bonds of all kinds have reached record levels in recent years. Early in 1982, for example, the United States Treasury brought out some new thirty-year bonds that returned a record initial yield of 14.56 percent. Only a few months earlier, the return on older thirty-year bonds issued by the Treasury had reached nearly 16 percent, and those on high-quality bonds issued by some of the nation's major corporations had changed hands at 18 percent. Although interest rates have since subsided considerably, they remain at high levels compared to what we have known in the past.

If interest rates are high, so are *real* interest rates. When economists refer to real interest rates, they mean the difference between the nominal interest rates on bonds and the inflation rate. Thus, if top-quality bonds pay 14 percent a year in interest and the inflation rate is 6 percent, the real rate of interest is 8 percent.

And 8 percent is exactly the level which real interest rates attained in 1982. Indeed, they were sometimes higher, depending on which month's annualized rate of inflation was used. The point is, a real rate of 8 percent or more is astonishing when you realize that historically this rate has been 3 percent or even less.

The reason real interest rates have surged to new highs is that investors have been unusually uncertain about what the future holds. As a result, they have demanded higher interest rates as extra protection against the unknown.

This uncertainty reflects another change in the bond market: unusual volatility in the prices of bonds, which in turn reflects unusual volatility in the growth of the nation's money supply and very high current and prospective deficits in the budget of the United States government.

As the interest rates and prices of bonds have become more volatile, the maturities, or lives, of bonds have become shorter. Historically, when investors have referred to long-term bonds, they have meant bonds with maturities of twenty, thirty or even forty years. Today many fewer such bonds are coming on the market. A very sizable proportion of new issues have maturities of ten years or even less.

There are at least two reasons for this. Corporations are reluctant to commit themselves to pay very high rates of interest for long periods of time. And investors are reluctant to tie up their money for such periods lest interest rates move higher, leaving them with smaller interest payments than they might otherwise have obtained.

There has also been an explosion of debt. Just between the start of 1976 and the end of 1981, the debt of nonfinancial corporations alone jumped from $600 billion to more than $1.2 trillion. And this trend is not likely to reverse.

All these things have been taking place at a time when the nation's corporations are under increasing financial pressure. Says Henry Kaufman, managing director of Salomon Brothers: "Our economy and financial markets are more fragile than at any time since the end of World War II."

Here's some evidence of what he is talking about: In 1981 the fixed-charge ratio of major corporations was only 4.2, down markedly from 4.9 and 5.5 in the two preceding years. This ratio measures the number of times a company could pay its interest and other fixed charges out of pretax income.

In this situation it should be no surprise that the credit ratings of many corporations have been lowered. These ratings provide a good indication of how safe it is to invest in the bonds or other fixed-income securities they issue.

In 1981 Standard & Poor's, an investment advisory organization that assesses the creditworthiness of corporations, states and cities, lowered its ratings on 167 companies and increased them on only 136. Among the companies whose ratings it lowered were some of America's industrial giants: Du Pont, Ford Motor, General Motors and RCA.

What has been true for business has also been true for many states and cities. Michigan, for example, has had the ratings on its bonds lowered. And the same fate has befallen the bonds of many major cities, such as Boston and Chicago. Indeed, some cities have even had their ratings suspended for a time while they tried to work out of financial difficulty.

These drops in corporate and municipal ratings have not generally been sharp ones, and they have not usually called into grave question the ability of the bonds' issuers to repay what they have borrowed. But they have been worrisome because the trend shows few signs of abating.

Thomas G. Fendrich, a vice president of Standard & Poor's and manager of its corporate financial department, predicts that the creditworthiness of corporations will remain under stress throughout the 1980s. Among other reasons: the declining competitiveness of American industry; turbulent economic conditions; lack of sufficient investment capital; high interest rates, and a big increase in corporate short-term debt, which must be paid off rapidly.

All these problems have helped create an atmosphere of uncertainty in the bond market, even though it was greatly buoyed by sharp rallies in bond prices in the latter half of 1982. And as if the problems weren't serious enough, they are continually exacerbated by an unprecedented amount of borrowing by the United States government and by continuing huge deficits in the federal budget. Indeed, these factors have been major causes of the problems just discussed, as the government has crowded corporate and municipal borrowers out of the bond market or forced them to pay high rates of interest on what they borrow.

In the present climate it might seem inadvisable to buy bonds. But plenty of experts would disagree. Says John Dighton, chairman and president of Roosevelt & Cross, an investment house that specializes in municipal bonds: "Over the long haul the period we have been in since 1976 will appear to have been a very fine time to have bought bonds."

Adds Albert N. Wojnilower, chief economist for The First Boston Corp., a leading investment banking house: "Bonds are still a great investment."

Common stocks, of course, have long been regarded as one of the best available hedges against inflation. Even so, they have never been a perfect hedge. Exhaustive studies done originally by the University of Chicago's Center for Research in Security Prices and recently updated by Computer Directions Advisors show that if an investor had bought all the stocks on the New York Stock Exchange at the beginning of 1926 and held them until the end of 1981, he would have enjoyed an average annual return on his investment, before taxes, of 9.1 percent.* This return would have included both appreciation in the prices of the stocks and the dividends paid on them, and it would have assumed that the dividends were reinvested.

This long-term return of 9.1 percent declined to 8 percent during the final five years of the period that ended in 1981. This is considerably below the average annual increase of 10.1 percent in the Consumer Price Index for the same era. And it is far below the interest rates that have recently prevailed on high-quality bonds.

A return of 8—or even 9.1—percent is not a sure return; it is the average return. And many investors did not do as well as the average, although they may have done much better in 1982, when the stock market flourished.

Does this mean that bonds are a better hedge against inflation than stocks? Not necessarily. Potentially, in fact, stocks are a better hedge than bonds can ever hope to be. Furthermore, investors who have bought bonds, then had to sell them before they matured, have sometimes lost more money than many stockholders. Then too, the high interest rates that bonds have returned in recent years have now fallen to a noticeable degree and may continue to do so, if not next month, then next year or the year thereafter. The prices of common stocks may rise almost across the board, as they did more than once during the second half of 1982.

*Whenever "he" is used in this book, other than in reference to a particular individual, "she" is also meant.

What all this does mean is that, as matters have recently stood, bonds have been a very viable alternative to stocks, demanding the attention of virtually all investors, institutional and individual alike. And not surprisingly, they have received it.

Life insurance companies, public pension funds covering state and local government employees, and private pension funds covering corporate employees purchased perhaps three quarters of all new corporate bonds issued in 1982. Other institutions and individuals bought the rest.

Indeed, individual Americans have recently been on a kind of bond-buying binge. In 1981, Salomon Brothers reports, individuals purchased roughly $50 billion worth of new federal, municipal and corporate bonds, an increase of more than 50 percent over the previous year.

Individuals were particularly active in the municipal bond market, where bonds issued by states, cities and their various authorities are sold. In fact, individuals purchased an astounding 74 percent of all new issues. This compares with a mere 19 percent in 1980.

To meet the increasing demand from individuals for bonds of all kinds, bond funds and other funds specializing in fixed-income investments have sprung into existence at a tremendous rate. It is almost impossible to keep track of them.

Together with the increase in demand for new bonds has come a marked increase in demand for bonds in the secondary market. Thus, once a bond has been issued and sold, it may be sold again and, if it is, the sale is made in what's called the secondary or after market.

Institutions in particular are much less apt than they once were to buy bonds and hold them until they mature. They are more apt to seek profits by buying bonds and selling them from time to time, just as they buy and sell common stocks.

These are some of the recent trends in the bond market. But what of the future? In particular, will the interest rates paid on long-term bonds remain at or near their recent levels, which have been high by historical standards?

Two observations should be made about long-term interest rates. First, a great many economists think these rates will remain high. Says George W. McKinney, Jr., an internationally known economist who until recently was chairman of the Economic Advisory Committee of Irving Trust Company: "Interest rates will be volatile and heading downward. But they will remain high by historical standards, even if inflation continues to moderate. Certainly they won't drop to the 6 percent level we once knew." Second, it seems likely that such economists will be proved correct as long as inflation and, perhaps even more important, fear of a return to double-digit inflation, remain with us.

As we have seen, the world of bonds today is an uncertain one. Yet it is also a colorful world, replete with its own language and ways of doing business. It is a world where "market in the shoot" means bond prices are dropping fast and "a blowout" signifies a new bond issue has sold out immediately, a world where U.S. Treasury bonds maturing in 2007 are known as "James Bonds," after the fictional hero also known as 007, and where U.S. Treasury bonds maturing in 2010 are called "Bo Dereks," after the voluptuous star of the movie *10*.

Let us now turn to what is likely to be of immediate, practical use to people interested in investing in bonds.

1.

The ABCs of Bonds

Bonds are widely considered the most conservative of all investments. To understand why, you need only understand the nature of a bond itself.

When an institution or an individual buys a bond, he makes a loan to whatever organization issued it. In return, the issuer promises to repay the loan at a certain specified date in the future and in the meantime to pay the buyer a guaranteed rate of interest.

A bond is, in effect, a promissory note or IOU. Whoever buys a bond becomes a creditor of the government, governmental agency or corporation that issued it.

The proof of the agreement is engraved on the bond itself. If you have ever seen one, you know that it contains a serial number, a principal amount, a date on which the principal will be repaid, an interest rate, and the name of the issuer.

How different, then, a bond is from a stock. When an individual buys a stock, he does not become a creditor. Rather, he becomes an owner.

The corporation whose stock he has purchased promises him nothing. Hopefully, of course, it will do well, increasing its earnings from year to year. In such case, the price of its stock is apt to go up, and it is apt to pay bigger and bigger dividends.

There is no guarantee, however, that this will happen. In fact, the reverse could take place. In such case, the price of the stock may plunge, the corporation may not pay any dividends on it at all, and its owner may find his investment worth only a fraction of what he paid for it.

Like a stock, a bond may fluctuate in price. If its owner has to sell it before it matures, he, too, may lose a great deal of money. But if he holds the bond until it matures, he will almost always get back the amount of money indicated on the face of the bond.

To be sure, a bond issue sometimes goes into default. In other words, the issuer is unable to pay principal, interest or both. But defaults are rare. And when they occur, bondholders have a prior claim on all the issuer's assets. As a result, the issuer must sell or otherwise dispose of its plant, equipment and other assets, then divide up the proceeds among its bondholders in accordance with what it owes them. Stockholders may get only a small part of the proceeds or even nothing at all. For this reason, bonds are sometimes referred to as *senior securities*.

If all this sounds as if bonds were an inherently better investment than stocks, it isn't necessarily so. If a company's profits soar, a stockholder is likely to benefit through an increase in the price of the stock, an increase in the size of the dividends or both. A bondholder, on the other hand, rarely benefits from rising profits.

All this is another way of saying that stocks and bonds are different animals. Each has advantages and disadvantages the other doesn't.

Who issues bonds? There are four major kinds of issuers. The first consists of corporations, and the bonds they issue are known as *corporates*. The second consists of state or local governments or other public bodies on the state or local level, and the bonds they issue are known as *municipals*. The third issuer is the United States government, and its issues are called *governments*. The fourth issuer consists of various agencies of the United States government and these bonds are known simply as *agencies*.

The government issues its bonds without much outside aid, and its agencies do so in a special fashion that will be described in Chapter 8. Corporations and state and local governments, on the other hand, issue bonds with the help of a special kind of banker known as an *investment banker*.

An investment banker agrees to buy an issuer's bonds and resell them to the public. In fact, he does a great deal more. He advises his client on how much money can be raised in the bond market and on what rate of interest will have to be paid. He also agrees to advertise the bonds and to arrange for their distribution throughout the country and perhaps overseas.

If a bond issue is very small, a single investment banker may *float* the issue. If it is very large, a number of investment bankers may join forces. In this case, they form a *syndicate* or *underwriting group*.

To give you some idea of the variation in the size of these groups, a syndicate of only eleven investment bankers recently announced that it was marketing nearly $119 million worth of bonds for the state of Washington. Only a few months earlier, a syndicate of no fewer than 190 investment bankers announced that it was floating $300 million worth of bonds for the Texas Municipal Power Agency.

Why Bonds Are Issued

Many times, corporations would prefer not to issue bonds; they would much rather issue stock. It is easy to understand one reason why when you recall that when a company sells stock, it commits itself to nothing. When it sells bonds, however, it not only promises to repay the amount it borrows, but also to pay interest along the way. In this sense it is more expensive to issue bonds than stock.

Nonetheless, at any given time it may not be feasible to issue stock. For example, the owners of a private company may not wish to share their profits with other owners. Or the company may be relatively unknown and stand little chance that a stock issue will be well received. Or the stock market may be relatively inactive and unhealthy.

Whatever the situation, companies, governments and other public agencies issue bonds all the time. In fact, they issue them in such numbers and such amounts that the bond market dwarfs the stock market many times over. In a typical year, the ratio of new bond issues to new stock issues may be five or even ten to one.

These organizations issue bonds for all kinds of purposes. They may wish to raise money to build a factory or to buy new equipment. Or to acquire another company. Or to pay off the creditors of older bond issues. Or to reimburse other creditors.

Sometimes a combination of reasons is involved. For example, some years ago TRW, Inc. issued $75 million worth of bonds to pay off long-term bank debt incurred in foreign lands, to pay off short-term debt incurred in this country and to redeem commercial paper (short-term IOU's).

Who buys bonds? Institutional investors, such as banks, charitable foundations, colleges, insurance companies, and pension funds, have long dominated the bond market. Of course, as we saw in the Introduction, individual investors have recently come forward in greater numbers than they once did.

Still and all, the bond market is basically an institutional market and is likely to remain that way for as long as we can foresee. Even in the aggregate, individuals do not have sufficient investment funds to meet the borrowing needs of the nation's corporations and governmental bodies.

Institutional demand for bonds is so great that an underwriter will sometimes tell a client that it can persuade just one or two big institutional investors to purchase an entire issue. When this happens, the underwriter is said to have made a *private placement*. In the past such placements have occasionally accounted for more than one third of the sales of all new corporate issues.

But usually an underwriter or syndicate buys the bonds from its client, then resells them to the institutional and general public for a slightly higher price. Sometimes an underwriter will negotiate the terms of such a deal with the client. More often, underwriters or groups of underwriters make competitive bids to underwrite a bond issue. In the latter case, the underwriter that enables the client to pay the lowest rate of interest wins the bid.

It is worth noting that in the future the role of the investment banker may decline, at least to a slight degree. This is because the Securities and Exchange Commission has authorized use, on a trial basis, of a regulation known as Rule 415 or the Shelf Rule. This rule permits a sizable number of companies to bypass investment bankers. All the companies need do is file a single registration statement with the SEC indicating the amount of bonds and stocks they want to put on the shelf, as it were, for issuance during the ensuing two years. They may then sell these securities when they wish and to whom they wish, saving on underwriting costs and red tape. Rule 415 has proved very popular with a number of major corporations in the early going, although for a variety of reasons some observers question how long its popularity will last.

Bonds are issued in certain *denominations*. These denominations may be as small as $100 or as large as $5,000 and occasionally many times larger. Ordinarily, however, corporate bonds are issued in denominations of $1,000. Thus it is usually assumed that $1,000 is a bond's *principal amount* or *face value*. It is the amount that the borrower will repay when a bond matures.

Curiously, however, bond dealers, magazines and newspapers do not list a bond's price at its face value, but at one tenth of this value. Thus a bond that sells in the open market at exactly its face value will be said to be trading at 100 instead of $1,000. Similarly, a bond that sells for $800 will be listed as trading at 80, and one that sells for $1,050 will be listed at 105.

Of course, bonds are often traded at fractional prices, just as stocks are. Usually these fractions consist of one-eighth, one-quarter and one-half points. If you see that a bond is trading for 98½, you will know that its price in the open market is $985 (98.5 times 10). Again, if it is trading at 98¾, you will know that its price is $987.50 (98.75 times 10).

The major exception to this statement involves United States government bonds, which trade in thirty-seconds of a point. In other words, if a government bond is trading for 70.24, it really means $70^{24}/_{32}$. That in turn means 70¾, which is the same as 70.75. This indicates that the purchaser bought a bond worth $707.50 (70.75 times 10).

A bond is normally issued to sell for its face value, which, as we have seen, is usually $1,000 (100). Thereafter it may sell for more or less. When it sells for more, it is said to be selling at a *premium*. When it sells for less, it is said to selling at a *discount*.

Nonetheless, not all bonds are issued precisely at their face values. Sometimes they are issued at a slightly higher or lower price. For example, in 1982 some bonds issued by the Columbia Gas System were first offered at 99.50. When something like this happens, it usually indicates that the underwriter had to bid more or less than normal to underwrite the bond issue.

Bonds are almost always issued for a certain length of time or *term*. A few are issued for a term of less than five years. Commonly, however, they are issued for from ten to fifty years. Historically, twenty- and thirty-year bonds have been the most prevalent, although in recent years many companies have issued bonds with shorter maturities.

The expiration date of a bond's term represents its *maturity date,* the date on which its principal amount will be repaid. During the course of its life, a bond may sell for a great deal more or less than its face value. But when it matures, its issuer will pay its owner whatever the face value is.

In practice, many bonds are paid off well before they mature. Thus, when a corporation issues a bond, it commonly states on the bond that the bond is subject to *call.* This means that the corporation may redeem the bond in advance of its maturity date.

Usually, the bond will not be callable before a certain date. For example, if the bond's term runs for thirty years, the corporation may promise that the bond will not be callable until at least five or perhaps ten years of its life have elapsed.

These days, most corporate bonds are callable. Sometimes corporations never exercise this right or only exercise it many years after they are first entitled to do so. At other times they exercise the right as soon as possible.

And when they do, they normally pay a premium above the bond's face value. In fact, when a company states that a bond is subject to call, it will stipulate the price it will pay to redeem the bond ahead of its maturity date.

Typically, a call price is equal to a bond's face value, plus its annual interest rate. Thus, if a corporation reserves the right to call in a series of bonds worth $1,000 apiece and paying 12 percent interest, it may promise to pay its bondholders $1,120 for each bond they hold.

At first glance, bonds subject to call may seem like a fine investment. After all, the bondholder will receive more for his bonds than if he held them to maturity.

On the other hand, the bondholder will no longer own the bonds nor receive interest on them. If his bonds are called in, he may give up 12 percent a year in interest and receive a one-time premium that is not likely to be much, if at all, larger than that amount and could be smaller.

Furthermore, a company may stipulate that its bonds' call price will steadily decline the longer the bonds remain outstanding. Take some bonds issued by Indiana Bell Telephone in September 1981. They pay interest of 17 percent and are due to mature in 2020. But they can be called as early as 1986.

If Indiana Bell redeems them in 1987, it has agreed to pay 113.99 percent of their face value, plus accrued interest. If it waits until 1997 to redeem them, it has agreed to pay 109.16 percent. If it delays until 2015, it has agreed to pay 100.48 percent. Thereafter the call price will equal the face value of the bonds.

Companies usually call in bonds because interest rates have declined sufficiently to compensate them for calling them in early, even though they have to pay a premium to do so. For example, a company may have had to pay interest of 15 percent when it first issued a bond series. But over the course of a few years, the interest commanded by new corporate bonds of its genre may fall to 10 or 11 percent. As a result, it may be much cheaper to call in the outstanding bonds and issue new ones at the lower rate of interest.

How Interest Is Determined

What determines how much interest a company will have to pay?

The most important determinant is the prevailing rate of interest on bonds of comparable quality. In other words, the organization that issues bonds will have to pay approximately what comparable borrowers have to pay if it hopes to attract any lenders.

This prevailing rate of interest is determined largely by the law of supply and demand. When there is a great deal of demand for money, the interest rate will tend to rise. When demand slackens, the interest rate will probably fall.

Yet this interest rate is also affected by the United States government. Through the Federal Reserve System, the government has considerable control over the amount of money pumped into the economy. If the Federal Reserve System increases the amount of money available, it makes it easier to borrow. As a result, the interest rate will tend to fall because supply will catch up with demand. If, however, the Federal Reserve System holds down the supply of new money, the interest rate will tend to rise because demand will probably exceed supply.

Actually there is no one prevailing rate of interest. There are several rates—both short-term and long-term.

One of the most important short-term rates is the *federal funds rate*, which is the rate banks charge each other for overnight loans. Another is the *prime rate*, the definition of which has been somewhat fluid recently, but which historically has meant the rate banks charge corporate customers of the highest quality. There are also several other rates of considerable importance, such as the rate on commercial paper.

These short-term rates do not always move in precise conjunction with one another. But they all tend to move upward or downward as the demand for money rises and falls.

Of the long-term rates, one of the most important is the *rate on long-term bonds*—those issued for terms of ten years or more. Another is the *rate on residential mortgages.*

Like short-term rates, long-term rates do not always move in precise conjunction with one another. Yet they also tend to follow the same broad trend.

But this does not mean that short-term rates and long-term rates always move in the same direction. Sometimes they do, and sometimes they don't. For example, in the week ending just before Thanksgiving 1982, the rates on U.S. Treasury bills and notes of up to three years' maturity all decreased various fractions of 1 percent, while the rates on U.S. Treasury securities of five to thirty years' maturity all increased like amounts.

Over an extended period of time, however, it is most unlikely that the two sets of rates will move in sharply opposite directions. Both groups are affected too markedly by the law of supply and demand not to respond in somewhat similar fashion.

Since World War II, the trend in interest rates that corporations have had to pay to issue bonds has been ever upward. To be sure, there have been downward tugs and hauls. Even so, in 1945 the most creditworthy corporations usually did not have to pay more than 2.5 percent to float a bond issue. Before twenty years had passed, they often had to pay 5 percent. By 1970 the interest rate on bonds of the highest quality had soared well above 9 percent. And recently it has been 12 percent or even higher. It has thus been extraordinarily high by the standards that have prevailed throughout most of this century.

The reasons for the steady increase in interest rates should be obvious. There has been a marked increase in inflation. There has also been an ever-increasing demand for capital by all branches of government, all kinds of corporations and all manner of individuals. The national economy may have suffered recessions and other ups and downs since World War II. But by and large, the nation has enjoyed a high rate of growth and a high level of prosperity.

To sum up, the going rate of interest on bonds largely determines what any given corporation or governmental body will have to pay to borrow money. Yet the going rate will provide only a ball-park figure. The credit standing of a bond issuer and its ability to continue to prosper will determine the precise amount it will have to pay. If the issuer is well known and well regarded and if its financial condition is considered sound, it may be able to pay considerably less than another issuer would.

How much less? Perhaps one quarter of one percentage point. Perhaps one half of one point. Perhaps a full point. Perhaps more. Although such differences may not sound large, they can add up to millions of dollars in interest payments each year.

Whatever interest a bond issuer agrees to pay, it promises to do so for as long as the bond issue is outstanding. If it agrees to pay 12 percent annually, you, the bondholder, will receive $120 a year for each bond you own. This will be true even if the bond's price fluctuates sharply over the years.

A Look at Yields

This brings us to another important facet of the bond market, one that is probably discussed much more frequently than interest rates or prices. This facet is known as *current yield* or *current return*.

Important as it is, a bond's current yield is not a separate entity, but reflects the relationship between the price a bond sells at in the open market and its interest rate. A bond's current yield may be exactly the same as its interest rate. Or it may be more, or less. Usually it is either more or less.

If a bond is issued at its face value of $1,000 (100), if it continues to sell at that price, and if its interest rate is 12 percent, then its yield will also be 12 percent. But if the bond rises in price, its current yield will fall. And if it falls in price, its yield will rise.

This doesn't mean that you won't continue to receive $120 in interest each year. You will. But it does mean that your true rate of return will be more or less than 12 percent, depending on what you paid for the bond.

It's easy to see why when you realize that a bond's current yield is determined merely by dividing its selling price into its interest payment. Thus if you divide a bond whose price is $1,000 into $120, you will obtain a yield of 12 percent. But if you divide a bond whose price is $900 into $120, you will obtain a yield of 13.33 percent. And if you divide a bond whose price is $1,100 into $120, you will obtain a yield of slightly more than 10.90 percent.

This brings up two important principles about bonds. Never forget them.

First, a bond's price and its yield always move in opposite directions. They never go up or down together. Inevitably, when one rises, the other falls.

Second, it should be obvious that when the prices of quality bonds fall and their yields rise, this usually has little or nothing to do with the nature of the bonds or with the creditworthiness of the organizations that issued them. Rather it reflects a rise in interest rates, a rise that tends to affect all bonds more or less impartially.

The prices of old bonds must fall when new ones carry higher interest rates. Otherwise no one would be interested in buying the old ones. So the old ones fall in price sufficiently so that their yields equal or at least approximate those on the new ones.

So far, as you know, we have been talking about current yield. But most bond experts believe a bond's *yield to maturity* is much more important.

Yield to maturity includes not only the interest on a bond but also interest on the interest, plus any profit or loss that will accrue when the bond matures. This profit or loss will represent the difference between the price you paid for the bond and its face value.

If you paid less than the face value when you bought the bond, your yield to maturity will be greater than the current yield. But if you paid more than the face value, your yield to maturity will be less than the current yield.

Take an example: A bond that will mature in ten years pays 12 percent interest. It currently sells for $1,100 (110). So its current yield is 10.90 percent ($1,100 into $120). But you will lose $100 of your $1,100 investment when the bond matures. Over a ten-year period, this amounts to a loss of about 1 percent a year. Yet yield to maturity also takes into account compound interest on the difference between the purchase price and face value for each year of the bond's life. So the exact yield to maturity will be 10.37 percent.

If, however, you bought the same $1,000 bond for $900 (90), the situation would be reversed. Then your current yield would be 13.33 percent ($900 into $120). Furthermore, you would gain $100 when the bond matures. When the interest on this $100 is compounded annually over a ten-year period, it pushes the yield to maturity to 13.88 percent.

But all this will hold true only if the bond is not called in before its maturity date. If it is called in, its yield to call date will be markedly affected. If it was bought at a premium, the yield to call date will be lower than it would be if the bond were allowed to mature. And if the bond was bought at a discount, the yield to call date will be higher.

As you can see, it is easy to figure current yield. It is much more difficult to figure yield to maturity.

Fortunately, there is no need to do so. Most banks, brokerage houses and libraries have standard bond-yield tables that show yields to maturity in accordance with maturity dates, interest rates and so forth. These tables can tell you in a jiffy what the yield to maturity on any given bond will be.

In addition, special-purpose desk calculators are now used to determine yields to maturity. They are programmed to calculate the yields when the user punches in known variables.

From what has been said so far, you may have assumed that when a corporation wishes to issue bonds, it need only locate an investment banker, agree with him on the terms of the issue, then wait for hungry hordes of investors to make their purchases. Nothing could be further from the truth.

A company that floats a bond issue is seeking a loan. As a result, an investment banker will usually investigate the company with great care before it agrees to underwrite its bonds.

The company may thus find itself in a position not unlike the one you might be in if you were to seek a loan from your local bank. If you are well known and well regarded in your community and if you have a good credit standing, the bank may be willing to lend you $1,000, $5,000 or even more, solely on the basis of your good name. In other words, it won't demand that you put up collateral as a guarantee that you will repay the loan.

Banks and other investors often take the same attitude toward corporations. The corporations are so big, so well known and so well regarded that, unless some special factor dictates otherwise, they can often issue bonds without putting up collateral. Bonds issued in this fashion carry a special name in common usage in the bond field. They are known as *debentures.*

In recent years, more and more industrial corporations have put out this kind of bond, which now dominates the field by a considerable margin. The reason for the trend is simple: A company's earning power is considered much better protection against the possibility of default than the right to take over its assets.

Sinking Funds

Whether they issue debentures or bonds requiring collateral, many companies state in advance that they will pay off some portion of an issue before it matures. To this end, they set aside a fixed number of dollars each year or else some percentage of the total value of the issue. They then use this money to call in some bonds, to purchase them in the open market or to make tenders for them—that is, to ask their owners to turn them in at a certain price. The money that is set aside is known as a *sinking fund.*

These days most companies that issue bonds employ sinking funds. For example, in 1982, Dayton-Hudson and Hospital Corporation of America both issued $100 million worth of sinking fund debentures—the first to mature in 2012, the latter in 2007. Obviously both companies will retire part of the issues before maturity. Dayton-Hudson, for instance, will begin doing so in 1988, retiring 4 percent of its issue that year and each year thereafter.

Among the usual reasons for establishing a sinking fund: The fund provides for orderly retirement of the debt and is looked upon with favor by the investment advisory organizations that rate bonds. In other words, these organizations are more apt to give a good rating to a bond with a sinking fund. This means that the issuing corporation will have to pay less interest than would otherwise be the case.

Whether or not they are paid off by means of a sinking fund, other kinds of bonds are backed by collateral. The best known of this group is a *first-mortgage bond*. This kind of bond is secured by all of a company's property, exclusive of its working capital. Sometimes the security includes not only all of the property the company presently owns, but also all the property it may acquire in the future.

Next comes the *collateral-trust bond*, which is rarely issued these days. When a company does issue a bond of this kind, it deposits common stock or other assets with a trustee to guarantee payment of principal and interest. Usually the value of these assets exceeds the value of the bonds.

Still other companies issue *income bonds* or *adjustment bonds*. In these instances, a company promises to pay interest on its bonds only if it earns enough to do so. If it doesn't earn enough to pay the full rate, it must pay as much as it can, to the nearest one half of 1 percent.

For example, it may have promised to pay 14 percent a year, only to find that it can pay only half of that. So it pays 7 percent. The next year, it may pay 5 percent or 10 percent or the full 14 percent.

Finally, there are *equipment-trust certificates*. These are issued almost exclusively by railroads and other companies in the transportation industry. The money raised by the bonds is used to purchase locomotives or passenger or freight cars or airplanes or ships. The equipment itself serves as collateral for the bonds.

It is worth mentioning that, although they are not referred to as debentures, all bonds issued by the United States government are just that. They are not backed by the White House, the U.S. Capitol building, the Lincoln Memorial, or any other property of the federal government, but only by the government's good faith and authority. The same is true of most bonds issued by states, cities and other local authorities.

The chief exception, as we will see more fully in Chapter 6, involves municipal bonds backed by a tax or by other specific sources of income. Even then, however, the bondholder has no right to seize a bridge or housing project should the issuer default. In other words, the lower-level governmental bodies do not put up collateral as that term is commonly thought of.

In essence, then, there are basically only two kinds of bonds: debentures, which are backed only by a company's general reputation and credit standing; and all other kinds of bonds, which are backed by collateral or, as in the case of income bonds, by a specific promise to pay.

It may seem as if first-mortgage bonds were the safest of all bonds. Nonetheless, debentures often make as good an, if not a better, investment. In other words, the nature of the issuing company rather than the nature of the bonds really governs the bonds' safety.

In addition to bonds, corporations, governments and other public bodies sometimes issue *notes.* In 1982 municipalities issued notes with a total face value amounting to approximately 37 percent of all the new municipal securities issued that year.

Like bonds, notes have a face value, return a stated rate of interest, mature at a specific date in the future and can be bought and sold in the ópen market. The chief difference is that notes are often issued for a term of no more than seven years—and frequently for much shorter periods. Bonds, on the other hand, are usually issued for longer periods.

Organizations sometimes prefer to issue notes rather than bonds because they do not want to commit themselves to pay high rates of interest over a long period. They hope that, when the notes mature, interest rates will have fallen.

Some organizations came to grips with this problem about a decade ago in a novel way. They began issuing *floating-rate notes.* These notes, which have been issued by various corporations and other organizations, are rarely, if ever, identical, but they are often similar. Their primary similarity lies in the fact that their interest rates are frequently tied to the yields on one or another security put out by the U.S. Treasury.

For example, in 1981 BankAmerica Corp. issued eight-year notes whose interest rates will change every two years to a level equal to 105 percent of whatever rate then prevails on two-year notes put out by the U.S. Treasury. The investor is further protected by a provision that allows him to redeem the notes every two years.

If you are to understand bonds fully, there are two other terms you should know: *bearer bonds* and *registered bonds*.

There was a time when bearer bonds were far and away the most common kind of bonds. These bonds usually had coupons attached to them, and the owner merely clipped off the coupons every few months and mailed them or took them to his bank, to the issuing corporation or to its paying agent. He was then presented with the interest due him.

It was long believed that bearer bonds were easily transferable. This was and still is true. As their very name implies, these bonds are assumed to belong to whoever bears or possesses them. But as you can guess, they are subject to loss through fire or theft.

There are still plenty of bearer bonds around, particularly among municipal bonds, where they have long been far and away the most common. But the day of bearer bonds is slowly beginning to pass. Since the midpoint of 1983, as a result of the Tax Equity and Fiscal Responsibility Act of 1982, virtually all *new* bonds of all kinds—corporate, municipal, Treasury and agency bonds—have been issued in registered form.

Actually, most corporations have long registered the

names of their bonds' owners on their books and on the bonds themselves rather than issue the bonds in bearer form. The corporations then mail interest to the owners as it falls due, usually every six months.

If you buy a bond, then sell it, you will be entitled to whatever interest has built up since the last interest-payment date. For example, if you own a bond that pays 12 percent in interest and you sell it three months after the previous interest payment, you will obtain 3 percent in interest—one quarter of the total interest due for the year. This kind of interest is known as *accrued interest*, and it is paid by a bond's buyer.

Where Bonds Are Traded

As of a recent date, more than thirty-one hundred bonds were listed on the New York Stock Exchange. Well over two hundred more were listed on the American Stock Exchange. Still others were listed on various regional exchanges, such as the Pacific Stock Exchange. Yet these bonds represent only a small portion of the total. The overwhelming majority of bonds are traded in the over-the-counter market.

This market, as you know if you have ever bought or sold stocks, is not a central market with its own building, organization, staff and so forth. Rather it consists of hundreds of dealers around the country who are linked only by telephone or more recently by the National Association of Securities Dealers Automated Quotation (NASDAQ).

The reasons most bonds are traded only in the over-the-counter market are quite simple. For one thing, it's much cheaper. Corporations can sometimes avoid hundreds of thousands of dollars in filing fees by not listing their bonds on an exchange. For another thing, it cuts red tape. Finally, unless a corporation is deliberately seeking a sizable number of individual investors, there is no particular advantage to being traded on an exchange. Institutional investors are not apt to be impressed with the prestige that supposedly accrues from an exchange listing.

This means, however, that you cannot always pick up your morning newspaper to learn what a particular bond is selling for. To find that out, you will have to call or write your broker.

Yet this is not so inconvenient as it may sound. That's because most individual investors do not buy bonds with the thought of selling them in a year or two, but with the thought of holding onto them for many years, perhaps until they mature.

Even so, bonds are sold from time to time, in much the same fashion stocks are. We will examine the details in Chapter 9.

What are the most important facts we have learned in this chapter? Five stand out.

A bond is, in effect, a loan to a corporation, government or other public body. The bond itself stands as the issuer's promise to pay back the loan on a certain date in the future and in the meantime to pay a guaranteed rate of interest that is fixed for the life of the bond. The amount of interest payable will be determined in part by the size of the demand to borrow money at any given time and in part by the credit standing and earning power of the issuer. More important than the bond's interest rate is its yield, which reflects the real rate of return on the buyer's investment. Finally, bonds are backed either by the credit standing of the issuer or by some specific collateral and are traded in much the same way stocks are, although usually in the over-the-counter market.

You can go a long way toward determining whether you have mastered the other information in this chapter by seeing if you can decipher the following bond listing, which is reproduced exactly as it appeared in a recent issue of *The New York Times*:

ATT   13¼   91   13.6   169   97½   97   97⅜   + ¼

Not sure of every figure? Here is an explanation:

The bonds were issued by American Telephone & Telegraph and pay interest of 13.25 percent a year. They will mature in the year 1991. At the time in question they had a current yield of 13.60 percent. On the day preceding the newspaper listing, $169,000 worth of the bonds were traded. The highest price at which they traded was 97.50 ($975). The lowest price was 97. The final price was 97.375. This represented a gain of one quarter of a point over the final price on the last previous day on which they were traded.

So much for the ABCs of bonds.

2.

How Bonds Are Rated

If you invest in common stocks, you probably do so with the help of a broker. If you use him regularly, he undoubtedly sends you various research reports published by his brokerage house. As you know, these reports discuss the merits of buying, selling or holding onto various stocks and usually devote anywhere from 25 to 2,500 words to detailing each recommendation.

If you ever invest in bonds, it's unlikely you will receive such comprehensive reports. Although they exist, most brokerage houses provide their clients with much sparser information.

For example, one report that recently crossed my desk listed fifteen corporate bonds. The report included only the following information about each bond: the name of the issuing company, the interest payable on the bond, the date it will mature, its rating, its price, its current yield, its yield to maturity, its call features (that is, when it may be called in and at what price) and its amount outstanding.

Of all such information, none is more important than

a bond's rating. This rating is designed to inform all investors, institutional and individual alike, of one thing only: how likely it is that the issuing company will be able to repay the money it has borrowed, plus interest along the way, and do both of these things on time.

Five organizations in this country rate corporate and municipal bonds and notes. The organizations are, alphabetically: Duff & Phelps; Fitch Investors Service; McCarthy, Crisanti & Maffei; Moody's Investors Service and Standard & Poor's Corporation. The last two organizations are far more important than the first three, and their ratings are more widely publicized, referred to and depended upon.

Just what are the ratings they issue, and what do these ratings signify? Standard & Poor's rates all bonds on a scale stretching from triple-A (AAA) through single-D (D). The significance of its ratings is as follows:

- AAA—Bonds rated AAA have the highest rating assigned by Standard & Poor's. Their issuers' capacity to pay interest and repay principal is extremely strong.
- AA—Bonds with this rating differ from AAA bonds only in small degree. Their issuers' capacity to pay interest and repay principal is very strong.
- A—Issuers of these bonds have a strong capacity to pay interest and repay principal. But they are somewhat more susceptible to adverse changes in circumstances and economic conditions than issuers of AAA and AA bonds.
- BBB—Issuers of these bonds normally have an adequate capacity to repay principal and pay interest. But changing circumstances or adverse economic conditions are more likely to weaken their capacity to make payments than is the case with higher-rated issuers.
- BB, B, CCC and CC—Bonds with these ratings are considered predominantly speculative in regard to

payment of principal and interest. BB bonds are considered the least and CC bonds the most speculative. In other words, although bonds carrying one of these four ratings may be of some quality and have certain protective characteristics, their pluses are outweighed by significant uncertainties about the issuers and by concern over their exposure to major risks under adverse conditions.

- C—Bonds with this rating are known as income bonds, meaning that their issuers have agreed to pay interest only when they earn income. When they carry this rating, the bonds are not returning interest.
- D—Bonds with this rating are in default. Payment of interest, principal or both is in arrears.

A Significant Division

If you have studied these ratings carefully, you will have noticed that the great dividing line involves bonds rated BBB. All bonds with higher ratings are considered safe investments for both institutions and individuals. All bonds with lower ratings are considered at least slightly unsafe. There is a strong speculative element to them and, unless you are an experienced investor and know what you are doing, most investment counselors would advise you not to invest in them.

What about the bonds right on the dividing line— those with BBB ratings? There you will get an argument. Some investment counselors would advise sticking only to bonds rated A or better. Others would say that if you use ordinary prudence, you can find plenty of bonds rated BBB that constitute good investments.

Some institutions limit their investments to bonds rated AAA, AA or A. Others limit them to those groups, plus the BBB group.

Both approaches are sound. Much depends on the

nature and requirements of the investor. The more important it is that he have virtually an absolute guarantee that he will receive payment of principal plus interest, the more apt he will be to stick to bonds rated A or better.

BBB bonds are the first to contain a speculative element. Those with lower ratings are clearly speculative to one degree or another. Naturally, they also pay higher rates of interest. But there is some question whether their issuers will always be able to pay this interest.

Standard & Poor's also adds plus and minus signs to some of its ratings—specifically AA through B. Thus a bond may be rated A+ or BBB−.

The addition of these symbols indicates the relative credit standing of the bonds. For example, bonds rated A+ are deemed slightly superior to other bonds with A ratings.

Moody's employs slightly different symbols than Standard & Poor's. When Moody's wants to give a bond the highest possible rating, it gives it an Aaa instead of an AAA. When it wants to give it the next highest possible rating, it gives it an Aa instead of an AA.

And so on down the line. Moody's Baa equals the BBB given by Standard & Poor's. And Moody's Ba equals the BB given by the latter organization.

Through the first six ratings—from AAA through B— the meaning of the symbols employed by Moody's and Standard & Poor's are the same or virtually the same. When Moody's rates a bond Aaa and Standard & Poor's rates it AAA, they have identical or very similar opinions of it.

Moody's, however, does not issue any ratings lower than C. So some bonds to which it gives ratings of Caa, Ca or C may be in default. Standard & Poor's ordinarily gives bonds in default a rating of D.

In 1982 Moody's began adding the numbers 1, 2 and 3

to its ratings of Aa through B. These are the same ratings to which Standard & Poor's sometimes adds a plus or minus. And the numbers serve the same purpose: They are designed to show the relative strengths of issuers whose bonds are given similar ratings. A corporation whose bonds are rated A1 is considered stronger than one whose securities are rated A2 or A3.

Although the two top rating organizations usually agree on the meaning of the ratings they employ, they do not always agree on how a given bond should be rated. Thomas G. Fendrich, vice president and general manager of Standard & Poor's corporate finance department, estimates that the two organizations differ on about one in every ten bonds issued by corporations.

Nonetheless, the ratings made by the two investment organizations do not usually differ by more than one grade. Moody's may rate a bond Aaa, while Standard & Poor's rates it only AA. But it would be unlikely for the two organizations to differ more strongly than that.

The reason their ratings are often the same and rarely more than one grade apart should be obvious. They both have access to the same statistics. These statistics tell a great deal about the issuer's ability to repay the principal, plus interest along the way.

The reason that the two organizations sometimes differ is that rating bonds is an inexact art. As Fendrich puts it: "Financial figures and ratios are the raw materials of the bond analyst. But they will not by themselves necessarily produce an accurate rating. At Standard & Poor's we make comprehensive evaluations of companies that are designed to cover all qualitative factors. These factors include, among others, the quality of a company's management, the quality of its accounting system and its financial flexibility."

Obviously, the rating a bond receives is very important to the investor. It tells him whether it is almost certain, highly probable or merely possible that he will get his investment back and be paid interest on that investment when he is supposed to be.

Yet this rating is every bit as important to the company or municipality that issues the bond, for the rating goes a long way toward determining how much interest the issuer will have to pay. The lower the rating, the more interest investors will want.

Take the spring of 1982. Suppose an industrial company issued a bond due to mature in ten years and that the bond received a rating of AAA. In such case the company would probably have had to pay interest of 14.75 percent, presuming the bond couldn't be called in for at least five years. But if the bond had been rated BBB, the company would have had to pay interest of perhaps 16.75 percent.

If the firm had been seeking $10 million, repayable in ten years, the difference in the two ratings would have cost it $2 million in extra interest over the life of the bond. If it had been seeking $100 million, the difference would have cost it a whopping $20 million.

What's more, when a bond receives a low rating, a company may not be able to market it at all. There simply may not be enough investor interest in it.

For example, in 1970 the Pennsylvania Company, the holding company for the Penn Central Railroad, wanted to sell $100 million worth of debentures due to mature in 1994. It was willing to pay interest of better than 11 percent, a very high rate at that time.

But before the bonds were brought to market, Standard & Poor's rated them BB. For that and other reasons, they failed to elicit interest, and the Pennsylvania Company never actually brought them out.

Even when a company can sell a low-rated bond, the rating will be a blow to its pride and perhaps its prestige, affecting all its efforts to raise money from other sources. Furthermore, the company's underwriting syndicate will have to absorb the loss on any portion not sold, making it less likely that it will want to do business with the company in the future.

Before examining how the investment advisory organizations make their ratings, there are several other facets of bond rating that you should understand.

First, the overwhelming majority of corporate bonds receive a rating of A or better. Standard & Poor's reports that in 1982 more than 70 percent of the some three thousand corporate bonds it evaluated were rated A or better.

Does it surprise you that the vast proportion of bonds receive high ratings? It shouldn't. Remember, we are not talking about a company's ability to become the biggest and most important firm in its industry, to open up sizable new markets or to treble or quadruple its earnings in a short time. We are talking about its ability to pay back what it borrows, with interest, and to do so on schedule.

A company that cannot pay interest on schedule is in trouble. A company that cannot pay back principal on schedule is in big trouble—it is bankrupt.

Changes in Ratings

Bond ratings are not necessarily forever. They can be and sometimes are changed.

When a change takes place, it does not affect the amount of interest the issuing organization must pay on the bonds it already has outstanding. But it may affect the prices of those bonds in the marketplace. And it will almost certainly affect the amount of interest the company will have to pay on future issues.

Standard & Poor's reviews all its ratings regularly. In recent years it has typically changed its ratings on about one in every eight corporate issues and one in every twenty municipal issues each year.

The ratings may go up or down. And within another few years, they may be changed back again.

For example, in 1965 Moody's slashed its rating on bonds issued by New York City from A to Baa. A year later, Standard & Poor's followed suit. A major reason: The city was selling bonds to pay for current operating expenses rather than for capital expenditures.

The downgrading brought cries of outrage from Abraham D. Beame, then the city's controller. He even called for federal regulation of the investment advisory organizations. But he got nowhere.

In 1972, however, Moody's pushed the city's rating back to A. A year later, Standard & Poor's followed suit, leading Beame to assert that it was only a first step toward a still higher rating.

Why the change in heart by the investment advisory organizations? There were many reasons. Among others, the city had consistently been able to overcome financial difficulties and seemed in a stronger position than it had been a few years earlier.

A few months after Standard & Poor's issued its new rating, the city brought out $362 million worth of short-term notes. Partly as a result of the change in rating, it saved some $2.1 million in interest over what it would have had to pay if the rating had remained the same.

Yet by 1975, only two years later, New York City was in extremely serious financial straits. It actually defaulted on some of its debt. And Standard & Poor's responded by suspending its ratings on the city's securities. For a long period the city found it impossible to issue long-term bonds, and it was able to obtain short-term financing only with difficulty.

In 1981, however, Standard & Poor's announced that it would give the city's long-term bonds a rating of BBB. It said New York had developed a coherent system of financial management and no longer relied too heavily on short-term debt to fund accumulated deficits.

Within three weeks the city brought out a $75 million issue of bonds due to mature over twenty years. The issue sold out within four hours.

Convertible bonds rarely obtain ratings of A or better. In fact, the majority of convertible bonds are rated BB or lower.

There are several reasons why. As we will see more fully in Chapter 5, convertible bonds are often made convertible into common or preferred stock because they would not be particularly attractive to investors if issued as straight bonds. Also, by their very nature they are more volatile than straight bonds, and their prices tend to fluctuate more frequently, rapidly and widely.

You should also be aware that the two major investment advisory organizations do not necessarily rate all bonds. Standard & Poor's, for example, does not rate bonds issued by the U.S. Treasury or various government agencies. It reasons that these are the safest of all bonds and, therefore, that other bonds should be rated in relation to them.*

Nor does Standard & Poor's rate bonds brought out by corporations that cannot provide audited financial statements. Or those that do not have demonstrable operating records. Or those that are not seeking at least $5 million for a given bond issue.

But these are exceptions. Moody's and Standard & Poor's do rate the majority of publicly issued corporate and municipal issues. But unless asked to do so, they do not rate privately placed issues.

The two big investment advisory organizations rate corporate and municipal notes as well as bonds. These notes are given the same kind of ratings the bonds are.

To make their ratings, the two organizations have a sizable number of security analysts, plus supporting personnel. At Standard & Poor's two analysts are normally assigned to analyze a given issue. They report

---

*Moody's does rate many, although far from all, Treasury and government agency issues. Specifically, it rates those issued directly by the Treasury or that are fully guaranteed by the government. Always, or almost always, it gives these issues a rating of triple-A.

their findings to five senior officers of the corporate bond department's rating group, and the five vote on what the rating should be.

Usually there is a strong consensus. When there is significant controversy, the issue is reviewed and the rating decided by the senior members of the rating group.

The Bond Rater's Task

How do the analysts go about rating corporate bonds? Obviously, they spend a great deal of time studying published reports about the company in question. For example, they pore over its recent annual and interim reports, the bond registration form it has filed with the Securities & Exchange Commission, plus historical information from the rating company's own library. On occasion they may also telephone the company's competitors or other trade sources. But more and more, they want to talk with the management of the issuing company. In 1981 they met with the representatives of some fifteen hundred companies throughout the world.

In making their ratings the analysts look at nine factors, according to Roy Weinberger, manager of Standard & Poor's corporate bond department. We will not examine all the facets of the nine factors that Standard & Poor's explores, only some of the more important.

The first factor is the strength of the issuer's industry within the economy and in relation to economic trends. Is the industry growing, stable or declining? Is it cyclical or contracyclical? Is competition regional, national or international? Is this competition governed primarily by price, distribution, product quality or some other factor? Is the industry heavily regulated by the government or not? Is it unionized and, if so, how vulnerable is it to strikes? Does it require frequent infusions of capital for plants and equipment, as the chemical industry does? Or, like the textile industry, is it more dependent on obtaining adequate working capital? These are among the questions asked.

Observes Weinberger: "Of the nine factors we look at, the strength of the industry is slightly more important than the others because the conclusions we reach will almost certainly set an upper limit on the rating to which members of the industry may aspire. In other words, no matter how well managed and conservatively financed a company may be, it is difficult to imagine us assigning its bonds a rating of AAA or AA if it is in an industry facing above-average risks."

The second factor Standard & Poor's looks at is a company's market position within its industry. It asks: What share of the market does the company have? How does this compare with its share in the past? What is its position likely to be in the future?

Next, Standard & Poor's looks at the issuer's past and present operating margins.* Is the issuer likely to improve these margins through more effective pricing or through cost-cutting? The investment advisory organization also studies the age and quality of the issuer's plant and equipment, the cost and availability of its raw materials, the presence or absence of long-term purchase agreements, the efficiency with which the company uses energy, and its labor situation.

Standard & Poor's pays considerable attention to management. It asks: How are its plans generated? How often are they checked and revised? How successfully has it planned in the past? What are its plans for the future?

The investment advisory organization also looks at

---

*A company's operating margin is derived by dividing its sales into its sales less the cost of goods sold (before depreciation), and its selling, general and administrative, and research and development costs.

management's financing strategies. It wants to know whether the issuer has reasonably firm targets for its capital structure; how cautious or daring it would be about stretching this structure by taking on new debt to complete a significant acquisition or major development; what kind of financing instruments, such as bonds, stocks, and commercial paper, it uses and in what proportions; whether it has specific rate-of-return criteria for new investments; and whether working capital and operational problems are quickly dealt with.

The fifth factor Standard & Poor's looks at is the quality of the issuer's accounting system. Weinberger says: "We want to know whether this system overstates or understates the financial performance and position of the issuer relative to its competitors, so we compare the company's accounting system with its industry's norm."

In addition, the investment organization looks at the issuer's methods of accounting for its inventory, its amortization periods, its research and development costs, its depreciation practices, and its future commitments and how well these commitments are funded. In general, it prefers companies that employ conservative accounting methods.

Next, Standard & Poor's checks the issuer's long-term earning power. To this end it studies the issuer's operating income as a percentage of sales and its pretax return on its average invested capital. Says Weinberger: "While the absolute ratios are important, it is equally important to focus on trends and on how an issuer's ratios compare with those of its competitors."

The investment advisory organization also looks at a company's earnings in relation to fixed charges, focusing on pretax coverage of interest and of interest and rents. It also probes various segments of the business to see which are strong, which weak, whether there are serious problems and what is being done to correct them. Finally, it ponders the likelihood that the issuer will be able to increase its earnings in the future.

The next factor studied is the issuer's financial leverage and asset protection. Standard & Poor's is primarily concerned with total debt as a percentage of the issuer's capitalization and also with how off-balance-sheet liabilities affect this ratio.

In addition, the investment advisory organization looks for assets that may be significantly undervalued or overvalued. Natural resources sometimes fall under the first category, intangible assets, obsolete inventory and uncollectable receivables under the second.

The adequacy of the issuer's cash flow is the next-to-last factor Standard & Poor's looks at. Says Weinberger: "We focus on the relationship between expected cash flows and projected capital requirements. We hope to get some insight into the issuer's future borrowing needs to see the extent to which debt repayments will be made out of cash flow."

Finally, Standard & Poor's considers the issuer's financial flexibility, which it defines as its financing needs, plans and alternatives, plus its ability to accomplish its financing program under stressful conditions without damaging its creditworthiness. How variable is the issuer's cash flow likely to be? How often will the firm have to issue bonds or stock? Will its bonds already outstanding mature in an orderly fashion and within a time frame that does not impose extraordinary demands on the company? Does the issuer rely too much on short-term debt? These are among the questions that are asked.

Weinberger emphasizes that no hard-and-fast formulas are employed in studying these factors. "Sometimes," he says, "financial measures heavily influence a rating decision. Other times the business risks faced by the issuer and other subjective evaluations are more important."

This, then, is how Standard & Poor's goes about rating a corporate bond. It is not easy. It requires evaluation of many factors, some of them subjective. Yet, as we have seen, most companies fare reasonably well in the ratings they receive.

In 1981, for instance, Standard & Poor's raised its rating on General Instrument's subordinated debentures from BBB to A. Among other things, General Instrument is the nation's largest supplier of equipment to the cable television industry, one of the largest suppliers of parimutuel racetrack systems, and a manufacturer of semiconductors for the telecommunications and information processing industries.

The investment advisory organization reported that General Instrument had dramatically improved its earnings protection in recent years by achieving strong sales gains in the cable television field. The company had also increased its cash flow, built up its supply of cash and internally financed some major capital expenditures. Hence the higher rating.

How Municipals Are Rated

In studying municipal bonds, which are put out by states, cities and various public authorities, Standard & Poor's looks at many of the same factors it considers in studying corporate bonds. Obviously, there are important differences between the two kinds of bonds. In fact, it·is probably more difficult to rate a municipal than a corporate bond. That's because there are more intangibles involved.

For example, there are no sales and earnings figures to look at, no profit-and-loss statements, no return-on-capital ratios. Furthermore, there are no competitive factors to assess. The state of Maine and the state of Washington may want to bring bond issues to market at the same time. But aside from this, they do not compete with each other in the sense that General Motors competes with Ford.

So Standard & Poor's has to look at other factors: What are the needs of the state or city issuing the bond? What is its debt per capita? What is the ratio of its tax-supported debt to the assessed valuation of its real estate? How adequate is its budget? How big a burden is that budget on its taxpayers? What is the area's outlook for industrial growth? Its outlook for population growth?

For reasons that will become clear in Chapter 6, municipal bonds are considered among the safest of all bonds. Nonetheless, not all municipal bonds get top ratings.

For instance, in 1974 the New Jersey Sports and Exposition Authority issued $302 million worth of bonds. The proceeds were used to finance the construction of a huge sports complex in the Hackensack Meadowlands. The complex includes a racetrack and a seventy-five-thousand-seat stadium for the professional football team known as the New York Giants. Revenue from the complex was expected to pay for the bonds.

But the Authority had to agree to pay interest of 7.5 percent to sell the bonds. At that time this was an unusually high rate of interest to pay on a municipal bond.

Furthermore, the investment advisory organizations were not overly impressed with the bond's other terms, and Standard & Poor's rated the issue BBB. A major reason: If the complex didn't generate enough revenue to pay off the bond's principal and interest, the New Jersey state legislature had made a mere moral commitment to step into the breach.

"A moral commitment," observed one Standard & Poor's executive at the time, "is hardly a legal guarantee. Administrations and legislatures change. Today's promise could conceivably go unhonored ten years down the road."

The project was later refinanced and now carries a firm guarantee from the state of repayment of principal and interest. The bond is now rated AAA.

This should give you a good idea of how investment advisory organizations go about rating bonds. The significant facts to remember are these: Two major investment advisory organizations rate bonds on a scale ranging from AAA through D, although Moody's does not issue any ratings below C. Most bonds receive ratings of AAA, AA or A and are considered safe investments. Many bonds with BBB ratings are also considered reasonably safe. Those with lower ratings contain a considerable speculative element. The lower the rating, of course, the more interest the issuer usually will have to pay. But ratings can be upgraded or downgraded. And when a rating is lowered, it may bring about a drop in the bond's price, although it will not affect the amount of interest that must be paid on the bond but rather the amount that will have to be paid on future bonds issued by the same organization.

You can go beyond the ratings. You can do your own research by studying annual reports, balance sheets and the like. If you become deeply involved in bonds, such research may prove wise. If you are a typical investor, however, further research will probably prove to be a waste of time. You are unlikely to uncover anything that the rating agencies don't already know or haven't already considered.

Nor is your interpretation of the factors that affect a bond likely to contain a greater amount of healthy skepticism. This is because the investment advisory organizations believe their responsibility is not to the corporation or municipality that issues a bond, but to the institution or individual who may consider buying it.

3.

Why Buy Bonds?

Why invest in bonds? Why, for that matter, invest in anything? Obviously, because you hope to make money. Because you think you will do better to invest what you have than to stuff it in a cardboard box or hide it under a mattress.

Yet there are people who probably should not invest at all. And there are other people who probably should not invest in bonds. How can you tell if you belong in one or the other of these two categories?

I suppose that every basic brochure on investments stresses that before anyone considers investing he should make sure he has enough money to cover basic living expenses plus some luxuries. In addition, such brochures usually emphasize that the investor should have adequate insurance, plus enough ready cash to meet major emergencies. In short, he should have a good-sized savings account.

But why not leave all excess funds in a savings account? Plenty of people do. And these days they have some justification. As this is written, many banks across the country are paying 10 percent or more in interest each year on certain special accounts.

Unfortunately, the money often has to be left in such an account for many months or even a few years. If it is withdrawn earlier, the depositor may pay a penalty that will reduce his yield considerably. Furthermore, there is no guarantee that banks will always pay these rates of interest. Finally, certain other investments may offer even bigger yields. Bonds are a notable case in point.

What's more, savings accounts offer absolutely no chance of achieving capital gains. So, in recent years at least, the person who has kept all his money in a typical savings account has lost ground to inflation.

All this is a long way of saying that although everyone should keep some money in a savings account, investors are well advised to invest funds beyond what they need for a rainy day. To what end? To make more money.

Three Investment Goals

Yet this answer is a little too simple. Historically, when people have invested money, they have tried to fulfill one or more of three basic purposes. These purposes are known as *safety of principal, liberal income* and *capital appreciation.*

Safety of principal means just what its name implies. Above all else, the investor wants to be sure that he will get his investment back at some specific date in the future. Perhaps he wants to get it back to educate his children. Perhaps he wants it back to establish an estate for his wife and family. Perhaps he has some other end in mind. Whatever his aim, he wants to take the least possible risk with it.

Liberal income also means what its name implies. The investor wants to obtain a very good return on his investment, a return equal to or in excess of the going rate. He cannot or does not want to depend solely on salary, fees or other earnings to pay his living expenses. Perhaps the investor is retired or for other reasons receives little or no regular income beyond pension or Social Security payments. Whatever his situation, he wants to supplement his regular income with income from an investment.

By definition, capital appreciation implies growth in the value of an investment. The investor may care little about safety of principal. He may be willing to risk the loss of his entire investment in the expectation that he will not lose it but rather watch its value increase twofold or fivefold or even one hundredfold in a few months or many years. He also may care little about receiving income from his investment. Instead he seeks to make his investment grow. He may need more money to buy a house, educate his children, travel abroad or build an estate for his family. Whatever his purpose, he seeks big gains in the value of his holdings.

These three goals are not necessarily mutually exclusive. In fact, it's rather easy to make an investment that promises considerable safety of principal and liberal income. It is almost as easy to make an investment that promises liberal income plus some chance of capital appreciation.

But, although it may be easy to fulfill two of these three goals at once, it is not so easy to fulfill all three. Even when an investor can do so, he will not be able to fulfill each goal to the degree he could if he concentrated on just one or two of them. He will not be able to achieve maximum safety of principal, maximum liberal income and maximum opportunity for capital appreciation at the same time. In other words, it is best to make one goal a primary end, another a secondary end and recognize that there will be considerable constraint on achieving the third.

How do bonds stack up against these three goals? Generalizations, of course, are almost always dangerous. There are always exceptions.

Yet it is an unspoken assumption of the investment world that bonds usually provide a great deal of safety of principal. As a rule, there is probably no safer investment, presuming the investor can wait until his bonds mature and does not have to sell them earlier for what could be less than their face value.

Bonds also tend to provide liberal income. They usually yield more than preferred stocks and common stocks, certainly more than most growth stocks.

Even when the yields on bonds are little or no higher than those on preferred or common stocks, bonds are regarded as more stable. As we have already seen, a company must always pay interest to its bondholders before it pays a penny in dividends to its holders of preferred or common stock. And even should a company pay a liberal dividend to its stockholders, it may slash this dividend or eliminate it altogether a few years later. It cannot, of course, slash or eliminate the interest it pays its bondholders.

On the other hand, bonds usually offer much less chance than common stocks for capital appreciation. As Frank P. Wendt, chairman of John Nuveen & Co., a nationally known dealer in municipal bonds, puts it: "There have been very few occasions during my thirty-five years in the business that the bond markets have provided spectacular profit opportunities. That is simply not the nature of our business."

Naturally, you may buy a bond that is selling well below its face value—for, say, $600 or $700 instead of the $1,000 it will be worth when it matures. If you hold the bond until maturity, you will reap a respectable capital gain. Yet if this capital gain is divided by the number of years you must wait until the bond matures, it may not seem quite so big.

As we will see more fully in a moment, you can also speculate in bonds, just as you can in common stocks or commodities. Speculation has been part of the bond market for as long as that market has been in existence.

It will continue to be part of the market for as long as we can foresee.

But to mention speculation is to beg the main point—namely, that unless you deliberately buy them for considerably less than their face value, bonds are not normally thought of as a way to enlarge capital, but to preserve capital and to obtain a good income from it.

Of course, if you invest in bonds that pay interest of 12 percent a year, you will double your money in about six years, assuming you reinvest the interest. If you invest in bonds that pay interest of 15 percent a year, you will double your money in less than five years. And obviously, you will achieve a return considerably better than the average return on stocks of 9.1 percent cited in the Introduction.

But again you beg the main point, for, if you invest in bonds that return 12 or 15 percent a year, you will give up the chance to invest in stocks that may appreciate at a much faster rate than 9.1 percent a year. You will take a safe capital gain and give up the opportunity to make a sensational one.

Setting Your Goal

To reiterate, most people invest in bonds not to make capital gains but to preserve their capital and get a good return from it. Should that also be your goal?

In investing it is important that you do not establish a goal that cannot be changed. A goal that may be entirely appropriate when you are thirty may be considerably less so when you are fifty and less so yet when you are sixty-five. If you are still young, you may want to seek capital appreciation above all else. As you grow older, you may consider liberal income or safety of principal much more important.

In short, at some point in your life, bonds may make a great deal of sense to you. And at almost any time, they are worth considering. For one thing, they can often serve as excellent collateral on loans and, for this purpose, are far more acceptable than stocks. For another thing, they can provide an important means of diversifying your investment portfolio.

No investor can expect all his investments to do equally well. The typical investor can expect to make money from some of them, yet lose money on others. So, if he is wise, he doesn't put all his eggs in one basket. He tries to spread his risk. He diversifies his holdings.

Some investors do this by investing in a variety of stocks. But the best investors and particularly the most affluent usually own a combination of stocks and bonds. The combination may vary greatly in accordance with general economic conditions and the needs of the individual. But as Samuel Thorne, a senior vice president of Scudder, Stevens & Clark, a well-known investment counseling firm, recently put it: "We suggest to many people with balanced portfolios that they keep 25 percent of their holdings in bonds and other fixed-income securities under any and all circumstances."

So far it may seem as if there were no dangers or drawbacks to investing in bonds, aside from the fact that they are not ordinarily considered the best means of increasing one's capital. Yet, like every other kind of investment, bonds do suffer from potential drawbacks.

For one thing, they can enter default. Between 1900 and 1943, the average annual default rate for corporate bonds was 1.7 percent of their face value. Between 1944 and 1965, this average annual rate slumped to 0.1 percent.* And it has not changed significantly since then. So the risk of losing principal, interest or both seems relatively small. And even this risk can be reduced by investing only in bonds rated A or better.

---

* See Thomas R. Atkinson, *Trends in Corporate Bond Quality*, New York, National Bureau of Economic Research, 1967.

Still, defaults on corporate and municipal bonds do occur. For example, some years ago the Chesapeake Bridge and Tunnel Authority issued three series of bonds, of different degrees of seniority, to help pay for the 17.6-mile combination bridge and tunnel that connects the Cape Charles area with Norfolk, Virginia. The Authority's Series A and Series B bonds have steadily paid interest. Yet its Series C bonds have been in default for many years and, as of early 1982, were behind in their interest payments by more than three years.

Furthermore, even when bonds avoid default, they are not entirely free of risk. Thus it may be your intention to buy them and hold them until they mature. But your circumstances could change, forcing you to sell. In such a case, there is a risk that your holdings may be selling for less than their face value.

Take an example. In 1981 alone, bonds issued by International Harvester, paying 4.625 percent interest and due to mature in 1988, plunged from slightly more than 70 to less than 31, a drop of almost 40 points.

Price drops of this magnitude are not common in the case of straight, as opposed to convertible, bonds. Yet they do occur from time to time, putting the investor who must sell such bonds at a tremendous disadvantage.

Another drawback to bonds is that they make a better buy at some times than at others. Although recent rates were high by historical standards, there is no guarantee how long they will prevail. They could fall (or rise even higher) at any time.

This does not mean that bonds may not continue to return a good income in comparison with other fixed-income securities. But it does mean that they may not be as attractive as they have recently been.

Remember, too, that the investor has to pay federal income taxes on the interest from all bonds except municipal (tax-exempt) bonds. This cuts into his yield.

Of course, he also has to pay federal income taxes on dividends from stocks. But when you remember that most people invest in bonds to obtain income and in stocks to obtain capital gains, you will realize that the tax on interest is more significant than the tax on dividends, although not necessarily more significant than the tax on capital gains.

Speculation

A substantial danger to investing in bonds, just as in any other investment, involves speculation. Naturally, speculation also offers the greatest opportunity for profit-making. Whether the potential gains outweigh the potential drawbacks is for you to decide. In any case, there are several ways you can speculate.

One involves trying to predict changes in the going interest rate and investing accordingly. For example, if you think that money will become more plentiful and that the interest rate will fall, you might buy certain long-term bonds. If the interest rate does fall, the price of bonds will have to rise to bring their yields into line with those of new bonds. You can then sell the bonds and reap a capital gain.

Predicting a change in the interest rate is perhaps not as hard as predicting a change in the movement of stock prices. This is partly because bond prices and yields are directly affected by the current supply of money, partly because there is a great deal of information available about the status of the economy, likely movements in the prime interest rate and other economic indicators. Still, making such a prediction is tricky. If the interest rate were to move upward instead of downward in an instance such as the one just cited, you could lose heavily.

You can also engage in a technique known as *sector swapping.* You may believe that certain kinds of bonds—

industrial bonds, utility bonds, United States government bonds or whatever—are undervalued in relation to other kinds. So you may sell bonds you believe are overvalued and buy those you think are undervalued. If the undervalued bonds rise in price, you can sell them and obtain a capital gain.

To engage in this kind of trading, however, you need detailed knowledge of the usual relations in price among various groups of bonds. For example, bonds issued by the United States government or one of its agencies ordinarily yield slightly less than the best corporate bonds. This is because the guarantee of the government or one of its agencies is considered better than that of any corporation.

Even so, issues of the government and its agencies occasionally dip to a level very close or even equal to that of top-flight corporate bonds. When this happens, it may be the time to buy the government or agency issues with the idea of selling them later on.

There are probably more opportunities to engage in sector swapping than in interest-rate anticipation. On the other hand, the capital gains from sector swapping are likely to be smaller.

You can also engage in what is known as *pure swapping.* You can swap bonds in the same category—for example, one corporate bond for another very much like it.

The bond market is composed of thousands of issues and, as interest rates fluctuate, not all bonds respond in exactly the same way at exactly the same moment. For a short period, there may be tiny differences in their prices and yields that ordinarily wouldn't exist. So you may buy bonds that seem behind in price or yield, on the theory that they will eventually catch up with the rest of the market. Usually you will be right.

For this reason, pure swapping is not a particularly risky technique. On the other hand, the gain on any single transaction is likely to be very small. Also, pure swapping requires a very detailed, up-to-the-minute knowledge of interest-rate movements and the reactions of individual bonds to these movements.

You can also buy bonds with relatively low ratings— say, bonds rated BB or B. If you do so, you will obtain a much higher rate of interest than you would if you bought bonds of higher rating. But you will be assuming that the bonds are much safer than the investment advisory organizations think they are and that the records of the issuing companies will eventually reflect this. If you are right, the bonds will probably rise in price sooner or later. Then you can sell them for a capital gain.

All of these techniques are employed by professional bond traders but are not to be recommended to most amateur investors. They require too much time and knowledge, and most of them involve a considerable amount of risk.

If you truly want to speculate, if you really are seeking big capital gains and if you can risk losing all you invest, you probably will do better to speculate in common stocks or commodities. The returns are apt to be greater.

Professional traders may protest that just as good gains can be made by trading bonds. And they may often be right. But the opportunities to speculate in stocks or commodities are more frequent. And for reasons we will learn later on, it is usually much easier to sell fifty or a hundred shares of stock or a commodity contract than it is to sell $5,000 or $10,000 worth of bonds.

There is yet another technique for speculating in bonds in the hope of making a capital gain. It is by no means risk-free, but it is probably the best method for the amateur investor to follow.

This method involves *leveraging*. Leveraging, of course, simply means investing with borrowed money. It is less expensive to leverage with bonds than it is with stocks because you have to put up much less money with bonds. You can borrow from 50 to 95 percent of the value of the bonds you wish to invest in; the exact proportion depends mainly on the kind of bond you buy. If you invest in stocks, on the other hand, you can currently borrow no more than 50 percent.

Here is a simplified, hypothetical example of how leveraging works: An investor wants to buy five bonds put out by American Telephone & Telegraph. They pay 3.875 percent interest and are due to mature in 1990. They sell for about 61. This means that their market value amounts to $3,050.

The investor puts up $610 of his own money—or 20 percent of the cost—and borrows the other $2,440 he needs. He pays annual interest of 16 percent on the loan. This amounts to $390.40.

Against this, he will earn annual interest of $193.75 (3.875 percent times the bonds' face value of $5,000). So his net annual outlay is reduced to a little less than $200, plus a very small sales commission, plus taxes on the interest from the bonds. These taxes will be negated because he can deduct the interest on his loan on his federal income-tax return.

Soon after he buys his bonds, the bond market rallies. Prices gradually rise about 10 points. So his bonds are now worth $3,550 instead of $3,050, and he sells them. He has made a small but neat profit of $500—less commissions, taxes and the annual net cost of his loan divided by the period of time he held it—on a total outlay of less than twice that figure. This, of course, is a commendable rate of return on any investment.

Let's look at a similar example on a much larger scale, suggested by Jon Martin Zayachek, a second vice president of Smith Barney, Harris Upham, a brokerage firm. It involves leveraging U.S. Treasury securities, a ploy that many investors find both within their means and exciting.

An investor purchases $1 million (face value) of U.S. Treasury bonds known as "Bo Dereks." They pay 10 percent interest, are due to mature in 2010 and sell for 72 ($720,000).

The investor puts up only $50,000 of his own money and borrows the other $670,000 from a bond dealer at an annual interest rate of 15 percent. This interest expense results in an outflow at a daily rate of $280. The 10 percent coupon, however, results in an inflow at a daily rate of approximately $274. Since the two cash flows nearly offset, the investor can concentrate on the issue's price movement, if any.

Let's assume the price rises from 72 to 77. This results in a five-point or $50,000 profit on an investment of $50,000, minus only the *net* cost of his loans and commissions.

Does this sound like the kind of investment that would interest you? Just remember that if the bond had slumped in price by five points, the investor would have lost his entire investment.

Bonds offer yet two other important ways of achieving capital gains. One way involves investing in so-called discount bonds, the other in convertible bonds. The first way is clearly safer than any of the speculative ventures discussed earlier in this chapter. And both ways offer decided advantages. They will be discussed in upcoming chapters.

Bonds Versus Stocks

So far I have largely discussed bonds as they relate to certain standards, such as safety of principal. I have not discussed them compared to other investments. Yet probably a few words should be said about the ordinary alternatives to bonds—common and preferred stocks.

Over the long run, common stocks offer a greater opportunity for capital gains than bonds do. At the same time, common stocks are ordinarily a far riskier investment.

But there is another facet to stocks that you should not overlook. They can and sometimes do return good income. Their yield is figured in the same way that the yield on bonds is, by dividing the price of the stock into its dividend. Thus, if a stock sells for $50 a share and pays an annual dividend of $3, it yields 6 percent ($50 into $3).

Unfortunately, the yields on common stocks rarely equal the yields on bonds. What's more, the yield on a common stock is much less certain than the yield on a bond. The dividend on the stock may be slashed or eliminated altogether. The interest due on the bond cannot be changed. Nonetheless, a number of companies in this country have paid dividends without interruption for many decades, and some have never cut these dividends.

Preferred stocks are a better bet than common stocks. Historically, in fact, preferred stocks have been the chief alternatives to bonds.

Like bonds, preferred stocks are considered senior securities. In other words, if the company ever goes bankrupt, its holders of preferred stock will be paid off before its holders of common stock, although not, of course, before its bondholders.

Like bonds, preferred stocks pay a fixed rate of return, which is called a dividend. And they usually carry a guarantee that their owners will receive this dividend even if the company's holders of common stock receive nothing.

Like bonds, preferred stocks tend to move in narrow price ranges. For example, during a recent twelve-month period, the price of the common stock of General Motors ranged from about 34 to 58, while the prices of its two preferred stocks ranged only 6 and 8 points, respectively.

Finally, like bonds, preferred stocks are rated by investment advisory organizations. The ratings on the two kinds of investments carry the same meaning.

So preferred stocks tend to meet the same two criteria that most bonds do, providing considerable safety of principal plus a liberal income. But preferred stocks usually offer little chance of capital appreciation.

If you are considering investing in corporate bonds, you should then look into the preferred stocks, if any, of the issuing companies. You can assume that the bonds are a little safer than the preferred stocks. And this is not only because bondholders have first claim on the company's assets in the event of bankruptcy, but also because the company may omit dividend payments to its holders of preferred stock in a given year or even for a series of years. If the stocks are cumulative preferred, however, the company will be required to make up the dividends in later years if it possibly can.

You will probably also find that the bonds yield more that the preferred stocks do. How much more will depend on the company and on conditions in the bond market. The figure may range from a few to many *basis points.**

Whether you should buy the bonds or the stocks depends on your individual investment requirements plus how the bonds and stocks stack up against each other in terms of safety and yield. All other things being equal, some investment experts think you should choose the preferred stocks only if they yield 1 percent more than the bonds. On the other hand, it's very easy to buy or sell, say, $2,000 worth of preferred stock, while it can be difficult or costly to buy or sell less than $5,000 worth of bonds.

What are the main things we have learned in this

---

* A basis point equals one-hundredth of 1 percent. In other words, 100 basis points equal 1 percent.

chapter? First, no one should invest in bonds or anything else unless he has sufficient money to live on plus
funds set aside for a rainy day. Second, bonds should
interest most investors, but at certain times in their
lives more than at others. Third, the great, lasting
attractions of bonds involve safety of principal and
liberal income. Fourth, it is possible to speculate in
bonds with an eye to achieving capital gains, but this
usually requires considerable knowledge of the bond
market. Finally, there are other investments that may
serve your purposes better than bonds at any given
time.

4.

Corporate Bonds: A Growing Boom

At the end of 1947, the volume of corporate bonds in the country's secondary market amounted to $14.1 billion. This figure includes only publicly offered, as opposed to privately placed, bonds. It includes only straight, as opposed to convertible bonds. And it reflects the bonds' face values rather than their market values.

By the end of 1982, thirty-five years later, this figure had soared to $500.6 billion. In other words, within less than four decades, the size of the corporate bond market swelled thirty-fivefold. Furthermore, there is no end in sight.

Why this huge increase in corporate debt? Largely because of rising costs and falling profits, many corporations are generating less cash than they once did. At the same time, their need for funds to finance construction of new plants and factories, to buy new equipment and to obtain more working capital is increasing all the time.

The rate of increase in publicly offered corporate bonds now far exceeds the rate of increase in privately placed corporate bonds. In the early 1950s, the volumes outstanding of the two groups were about equal. But a gap soon began to appear, and it has slowly become wider and wider. As a result, in recent years a great many more publicly offered as opposed to privately placed bonds have come to market.

The public market at any one time offers thousands of issues. These issues vary greatly in interest rates, maturity dates and other factors. They also vary according to industry.

Salomon Brothers reports that the market is dominated by utility issues. At the end of one recent year these issues accounted for about 51 percent of the total volume of corporate bonds. Next came industrial bonds, with nearly 28 percent, then finance bonds, with about 17 percent and finally transportation bonds, with 4 percent.

The reason utilities dominate the market is quite simple. Their demand for capital to finance new construction and new equipment is tremendous and never-ending regardless of how profitable they may be in any given period.

From the investor's standpoint, this dominance is good. Although most bonds receive high ratings from the investment advisory organizations, utility bonds tend to receive the highest of all.

How to Pick a Bond

Obviously, however, there are many other very good corporate bonds around. How should you pick among them? We have already discussed or touched upon three or four of the most important factors to consider.

One, of course, is safety of principal. You can go a long way toward determining a bond's safety of principal by ascertaining its credit rating. As you know, a bond with a rating of AAA, AA or A is considered very safe.

Another factor is yield. In all probability, you will want the highest possible yield. Presumably you will also want maximum safety of principal. Yet the higher a bond's rating, the lower its yield is apt to be. So you will have to compromise. Even so, the compromise will not have to be that drastic. You can find many bonds with very considerable safety of principal and very good yields, even though they may not provide the greatest possible degree of each.

The third factor to consider is maturity. You may be willing to invest your money for a long period of time— say, the twenty or thirty years for which many bonds are issued. Or you may want to invest for a much shorter period—say, ten years.

If you want to buy a brand-new bond, its maturity date will have a definite effect on its interest rate and yield. The farther the maturity date is in the future, the more interest the bond will be apt to pay, at least when normal market conditions prevail. This is because the issuer will have use of the money it borrows for a longer period of time.

To cite an example, Commonwealth Edison recently issued two series of first-mortgage bonds on the same day. Each issue was worth $100 million. The first issue, due to mature in 1992, pays interest of 14.25 percent. The second, due to mature twenty years later, pays 15.375 percent.

Of course, you don't have to buy new bonds. You can buy those that have been traded for some period of time and that are due to mature in seven years or eleven years or at the end of some other period in the future. The interest rates on these bonds also will have been set partly in terms of their maturity dates. But the fact that you may buy them several years after they were issued will have no effect on the interest you receive, although it may, of course, affect the yield.

The final factor to consider is a bond's call provisions.

There was a day when only a minority of corporate bonds had such provisions. But all that has changed since World War II. Today most new bonds are callable after a specified period of time.

Naturally, the issuing companies don't always exercise this option. But when they don't, it is usually because they will not be able to issue new bonds at a lower rate of interest. They will have to pay the same rate or one that is even higher.

This brings up the one great disadvantage that utility bonds suffer in relation to other corporate bonds. Most, although not all, utility bonds can be called in after five years. Most, although not all, corporate bonds can be called in only after ten years.

Whatever the exact terms of a bond's call provisions, they usually place a ceiling on the price to which a bond may rise in the open market. In other words, investors are usually unwilling to pay more for a bond than its call price.

Nonetheless, call provisions are probably here to stay. So if you want to invest your money for ten years, be cautious about purchasing a bond that can be called in in five. Or if you want to invest your money for five years, be careful about purchasing a bond that has already been trading for two years and that can be refunded in another three.

All these factors—safety, yield, maturity and call provisions—should probably be weighed separately rather than together. In so doing, you will rapidly reduce the size of the bond universe. Even so, you will find a wealth of bonds to choose from.

If you confine yourself to bonds rated AAA, you will still be able to find many in that category with different yields, maturities and call provisions. Or, if you confine yourself to bonds yielding, say, 13 percent or more, you will still be able to find many with different ratings, maturities and call provisions.

There is a special kind of corporate bond that may,

and probably should, interest you very much. It's known as a *discount bond*. And as its very name implies, it is a bond that sells at a discount from its face value. As you know, this value is usually $1,000 (100).

Do not assume, however, that all bonds selling at discounts are discount bonds as that term is commonly used. At various times, many bonds sell at discounts merely because bond prices in general are depressed. Others sell at discounts because some question has arisen as to whether the issuing corporations will really be able to pay them off when they mature.

A true discount bond is a special breed of cat. Often it is an older bond that pays a very low rate of interest, perhaps only 4 or 5 percent, or even less. Often, too, it is due to mature in only three or four years.

Most such bonds were issued years ago. But as time passed, interest rates rose substantially. As a result, the older bonds had to drop in price. Otherwise their yields wouldn't have matched the yields on the newer bonds, and they wouldn't have aroused much interest among investors.

This brings up the first and greatest advantage of discount bonds. They provide an opportunity for capital gain. Furthermore, barring default, the opportunity for capital gain is a sure-fire thing, involving no speculation whatsoever.

Discount bonds provide this opportunity because the corporations that issued them will eventually have to pay them off at their face value. Thus, if you invest in discount bonds before they mature, you will reap the difference between the discounted price you pay for them and their face value.

Furthermore, this gain can be treated as a capital gain. As you know, this means that it will be subject to much lower taxes than interest and other ordinary income are.

Not all discount bonds are due to mature in only a few years. Some may not mature for ten years or more. But they differ from other bonds that may be selling at a discount in that they were issued when interest rates were considerably lower.

For example, Cleveland Electric has some discount bonds outstanding that will mature in 1994. They pay interest of 4.375 percent and, as this is written, were selling for a little less than 46.

You may wonder how much chance there is that such a bond will be called in. The chance is slight. A corporation is not likely to call in a bond that is selling at a sizable discount, because it would have to pay it off at its face value. It would thus lose the money it had borrowed. And if it had to borrow more, it would undoubtedly have to pay substantially greater interest.

The closer a discount bond approaches its maturity date, the more it is apt to rise in price. Everybody knows that when it matures it will be worth its face value.

To look at the whole matter another way, if you want to seek capital gains, you will be better off to buy discount bonds that won't mature for a number of years than to buy those that will mature in only one or two years. The farther off a discount bond's maturity date is, the deeper its discount is apt to be.

A case in point: Some Exxon bonds, paying 6 percent and due to mature in 1997, were selling in the summer of 1982 for 53. But some Du Pont bonds, paying exactly the same interest and due to mature in 2001, were selling for 45.

Observes Frank P. Wendt, chairman of John Nuveen & Co.: "Never overlook discount bonds. They have extraordinary potential for capital gain when long-term interest rates decline and prices rise. They provide the additional advantage of protection against being called in. Therefore, the potential for gain is not held down by an early refunding date or a relatively low price."

Are there no drawbacks to discount bonds? Certainly there are.

For one thing, you may not buy them near the bottom

of the market. After your purchase, interest rates may rise, pushing down bond prices farther. If you had delayed your purchase, you might have been able to buy the bonds at an even lower price and thus increased the amount of your potential capital gain. Thus timing is important to the purchase of discount bonds, just as it is to almost every other kind of investment.

What's more, you should not consider discount bonds if your primary investment goal is liberal income. By definition, discount bonds pay less interest than other kinds of bonds.

Finally, for all practical purposes there is a limit on the amount of capital gain you can achieve by investing in discount bonds. That limit is equal to their face value, for a bond of this kind is not apt to rise much, if at all, above that value.

If you are primarily interested in capital gains, you may do better to invest in common stocks. The potential will be greater, possibly much greater, although it's only fair to add that you could end up suffering a loss instead of achieving a gain.

The real strength of discount bonds is that the capital gains they offer are virtually assured. Common stocks offer nothing so certain.

New Kinds of Bonds

In very recent years a number of new kinds of bonds have come on the market. Three of the most widely publicized are known as original issue discount bonds, zero coupon bonds and put, or option tender, bonds.

As their name indicates, *original issue discount bonds* are priced from the start at deep discounts from their face values. As a result, they return much lower rates of interest than conventional bonds of comparable maturity.

Although a number of other well-known corporations have since followed suit, Martin Marietta first introduced this kind of security in 1981. Its thirty-year issue was priced at $538.35 instead of $1,000 and carried an interest rate of 7 percent. Yet because of its low price and the capital gain it promised at maturity, the bond offered a yield to maturity of 13.25 percent.

This yield to maturity was a bit lower than those on conventional bonds of comparable maturity, which is a major reason why original issue discount bonds appeal to corporations like Martin Marietta that issue them. Corporations can get away with offering slightly lower yields because these bonds provide other benefits to certain institutional investors.

Hard on the heels of the original issue discount bond came its close cousin, the *zero coupon bond*. This bond pays no interest at all. Its entire appeal lies in the capital gain the investor receives at maturity, which is why some brokerage houses promote it as a "money multiplier note."

To give you an example of how these bonds work, J. C. Penney brought out a $200 million, eight-year issue in 1981. The initial offering price on each bond was $332.50, and the initial yield to maturity was 14.25 percent, slightly below the rate on conventional bonds of like maturity.

Both original issue discount and zero coupon bonds have certain advantages. For one thing, it is extremely unlikely that they will be called in early. Corporations are just not apt to call in bonds on which they are paying low rates of interest—or no interest at all. For another thing, the bonds promise capital gains.

Unfortunately, this is not the whole story, for both original issue discount and zero coupon bonds suffer from several serious disadvantages as far as the individual investor is concerned. The biggest is this: Each year the individual investor must pay tax on income he does not receive—that is, on some part of the difference between the price he paid for the bond, perhaps $350 or $400, and its face value of $1,000.

Furthermore, he is taxed at the ordinary income tax rate, not the capital gains rate. Then, too, as we have already seen, the yields to maturity on original issue discount and zero coupon bonds are somewhat lower—usually 50 to 100 basis points lower—than those on conventional bonds. These are big drawbacks.

Indeed, these bonds appeal, and should appeal, most strongly to certain institutional investors such as public and private pension funds that do not have to pay taxes. They should have no appeal to individual investors who want income, and extremely little appeal even to individual investors who do not need such income.

The major exception to this statement involves individuals who want to buy such bonds for individual retirement accounts (IRAs) and Keogh plans or for custodial accounts for young children. Income can accumulate tax-free in IRAs and Keoghs until their owners retire. Children usually owe no taxes or, if they do owe them, are taxed at very low rates.

Even if you intend to buy bonds for such investment vehicles as these, however, you should look into regular discount bonds—those whose prices have fallen because interest rates have risen—before plunging into original discount or zero coupon bonds. For a variety of reasons, including possibly higher yields to maturity, some experts think regular discounts often may be more appealing.

Probably the most interesting new kind of bond to come on the market is the *put bond*. These bonds differ from all other bonds in that their owners may cash them in for their full face value well before they mature. Sometimes the owners are given only one chance to do so, on a given date only a few years after the bonds are issued. At other times the owners may redeem the bonds annually.

This right gives investors an opportunity to hedge their bets. They do not have to tie up their money for long periods and run the risk that interest rates will rise significantly above the rates they are receiving. They can cash in their bonds early and reinvest at the higher rates.

For this privilege, they pay a penalty. The interest rates on corporate put bonds are apt to be slightly lower than those on conventional bonds issued at the same time and carrying the same rating.

Sometimes these rates are fixed. At other times they fluctuate. In the latter cases the rates are often tied to the return on three-month or six-month U.S. Treasury bills. Usually they float about 1 percent above the rates on these bills and have a floor beneath which they will not be allowed to fall.

Put bonds carry an additional advantage: If interest rates rise, the bonds are not likely to fall as far in price as conventional bonds. This is because they can be cashed in early.

In sum, these bonds have definite appeal to many investors. Even so, carefully examine any you consider buying. One reason: The conditions under which they may be put—cashed in—can vary markedly from bond to bond. In some cases, you may have to state your intentions months in advance.

In 1982 a number of major corporations began bringing out a brand-new kind of security known as an *extendable note*. It is a substitute for long-term bonds, which many corporations did not wish to issue during this period because they would have committed themselves to paying high rates of interest for many years to come.

The exact terms of these notes vary. But the gist of them is this: They allow the buyers of the notes either to demand full payment of principal after a brief number of years or to hold onto the notes at a new rate of interest set by formula in advance. Sometimes the issuers are allowed to redeem their notes at certain set periods, too.

For example, in July 1982 Federated Department

Stores issued $150 million in extendable notes, paying 14.50 percent interest. Buyers may cash the notes in in 1985, 1988, 1991 or 1994. Or they may extend them in those years, when their coupon rate will be reset at a level not less than 102 percent of the rate on new three-year U.S. Treasury notes. Conversely, Federated may redeem the notes in 1984, 1987, 1990 or 1993.

The list of new kinds of bonds could be extended. For example, there are now bonds with warrants attached. The warrants permit the bonds' buyers to purchase additional bonds on the same terms as they made their original purchases. Then there are bonds backed by a commodity such as gold or silver. For instance, Sunshine Mining has fifteen-year bonds outstanding that are redeemable at maturity for either $1,000 or the dollar value of fifty ounces of silver, whichever is greater. The interest they pay is considerably lower than that on conventional bonds of similar quality and maturity. Thus like the other new bonds discussed, bonds with warrants and bonds backed by a commodity have both advantages and disadvantages. You should not buy any of these new securities without understanding them fully.

What are the most important things we have learned in this chapter? First, the corporate bond market has been growing at a very rapid rate and is almost certain to continue to do so throughout this decade. Second, corporate bonds are available for investment in a wide range of ratings, yields, interest rates and maturity dates. Third, corporate bonds selling at discounts from their face values offer the possibility of almost sure-fire capital gains. Fourth, several important new kinds of bonds have come on the market in the past few years. Individual investors should examine them closely before buying them.

5.

Convertible Bonds: The Ideal Investment?

There is an old saying that convertible bonds make the ideal investment. Like all old sayings, it contains an element of truth. And like all old sayings, it is subject to many qualifications.

The reason convertible bonds are often called the ideal investment lies in their nature. They can be converted into a specific number of shares of stock—usually common, although sometimes preferred. They are, in a way, part bond and part stock.

In theory at least they are believed to partake of the best of both worlds. In bull markets they are supposed to act like stocks and enjoy rises in price. In bear markets they are supposed to act like bonds and resist declines in price.

Often enough this theory works out. For example, between January and June 1982 General Host's common stock rose in price more than 48 percent, while its convertible bonds went up more than 17 percent. Similarly, during the same period, Hughes Tool's common stock plunged 51 percent, while its convertible bonds dropped only a little more than 16 percent.

Nonetheless, the theory often proves erroneous, at least to some degree. As in the case of General Host, convertibles sometimes go up nowhere nearly as fast as their related common stocks. And on occasion convertibles fall in price even more precipitously.

Even at their best, convertibles are subject to much wider price fluctuations than regular bonds are. For example, in a twelve-month period ending in mid-1980 Avco convertibles of 1993 ranged from 73 to 50, finishing at 60. And Trans World Airlines convertibles of 1994 varied from 62 to 36½, ending slightly above 44.

Still wider fluctuations could be cited. The point is that price swings of this magnitude are not considered unusual among convertible bonds. But they are considered unusual among regular bonds of good quality.

Before proceeding further, let's learn more exactly what convertibles are and why they act as they do. Unfortunately, they are one of the hardest of all investments to understand; fortunately, we already know a great deal about them. That's because they have many of the same features as regular bonds.

For example, convertible bonds have a face value, which usually is $1,000. Yet it is commonly listed as 100.

Convertibles also pay a fixed rate of interest. Because they are convertible, however, this rate is almost invariably less than what it would be on a regular bond issued by the same company at the same time. The difference may range from less than one to several percentage points.

These bonds also have maturity dates, at which time they may be redeemed for their face values, no matter at what prices they have traded in the meantime. Although the terms of convertibles vary widely, they generally run from fifteen to twenty-five years.

In addition, convertibles usually carry call prices. These prices are somewhat in excess of the bonds' face values.

Finally, convertible bonds have an *investment value*.

This term refers to the price a convertible bond would probably sell at if it were merely a bond and not a bond that was convertible into stock—that is, the price it would sell at on the basis of yield alone.

Unlike face values, interest rates, maturity dates and call prices, investment values are not immutably fixed, nor are they made part of convertible bonds' indenture provisions. Rather they represent the best estimates of investment advisory organizations such as Moody's and Standard & Poor's. These estimates are based on credit ratings, interest rates and other factors. Because these ratings and rates sometimes change, investment values sometimes do too, moving either upward or downward.

Why is a convertible's investment value important?

For one thing, the difference, if any, between a bond's market price and its investment value is an important factor to consider in deciding whether the bond would make a sound investment. The larger the difference, the less protection the bond will provide against a fall in price.

For another thing, a bond's investment value is supposed to provide a floor beneath its price. After all, this value is set largely in terms of what other bonds of comparable stature sell for.

Yet to say that the floor usually holds up is not to say that it always does so. If the issuing company defaults on interest payments or if the Federal Reserve System takes action that increases interest rates, a bond's price may dip below its investment value, in which case the value may change.

The Right to Convert

As we have noted, a convertible bond carries a special right: the right to convert it into a specified number of shares of the issuing company's preferred or common stock. Thus the bond may be convertible into five or fourteen or twenty-three or some other number of shares of stock. Whatever the exact number, it constitutes the bond's *conversion ratio.*

Typically, this right extends throughout the life of the bond and remains constant throughout that life. But there are exceptions to this rule and, if you ever consider investing in such bonds, you should familiarize yourself with their conversion terms.

Occasionally, a bond can't be converted until several months or years after it has been issued. More often, it is convertible into steadily smaller amounts of stock. For example, it may be convertible into fifteen shares of stock over the first ten years of its life, ten shares over the next five, and five shares over the last five. Sometimes the conversion privilege expires altogether before the bond matures.

The value of the number of shares for which a convertible can be exchanged gives it a *conversion value,* which is not to be confused with its conversion ratio. The conversion value is equal to the price of the company's stock multiplied by the number of shares for which the bond may be exchanged. For example, if the stock is selling at 50 and each bond is convertible into five shares, the bond's conversion value is 250 (five shares times $50 a share).

A bond's conversion value is important for several reasons. First, it increases when the price of the common stock increases, thus pulling the price of the bond upward in a bull market. Simple arithmetic shows why. If the price of the stock mentioned above were to increase from 50 to 75, the conversion value of the bond would have to go up proportionately, to 375 (five shares times $75). Second, a bond will rarely sell for less than its conversion value. In fact, it will usually sell for more.

In short, the difference, if any, between a bond's market price and its conversion value will be another important factor in deciding whether it would make a sound investment. The larger the difference, the less potential the bond will have for increasing in price.

This difference, if any, is known as the *conversion premium* and is often expressed as a percentage. As this is written, Piedmont Airlines' convertible bonds of 2007 have a conversion premium of 20 percent, representing the difference between the market price of the bonds and the value of the shares of stock into which they may be converted.

Thus we have three conversion terms: conversion ratio, referring to the number of shares into which a bond may be converted; conversion value, referring to the value of the shares into which it may be converted; and conversion premium, referring to the difference between the bond's market price and its conversion value.

Why do companies issue convertible bonds?

Sometimes they issue convertibles because they aren't able to bring out a bond issue in any other fashion. Perhaps they already have a lot of conventional bonds outstanding. Another might make a glut on the market. Or perhaps the market is temporarily unreceptive to new bond issues. Or perhaps investors have reservations about the soundness of the issuers. In the latter two cases, the conversion privilege provides a sweetener. It makes the bonds more attractive than they otherwise would be.

Sometimes companies issue convertibles because they can pay lower rates of interest than they would have to pay on straight bonds. Over the years, the difference in rates may save millions of dollars.

Sometimes companies issue convertibles because they hope buyers will eventually convert them into stock. In such case, the companies will no longer have any debt to pay off. Bondholders will become stockholders. It is no problem to make the exchange. Brokers handle the job routinely.

Indeed, corporations have been known to force their bondholders to convert. As we will see more fully in a moment, a company is in a position to do this when its convertible is selling for considerably more than its call price. Bondholders who don't convert or sell their holdings may lose a great deal of money.

Finally, and most important, companies sometimes issue convertibles because they don't want to issue common stock. Perhaps they don't want to dilute the value of the common stock they already have outstanding by issuing more shares. Or perhaps they don't want to pay the dividends they would probably have to pay if they issued stock. The interest on bonds can be deducted before corporate taxes are computed. The dividends on stock must be paid out of post-tax income. The difference can be substantial.

For all these reasons, the convertible bond market is popular. Certainly it is a market that should interest you.

You might be interested in it because you want more protection than you would obtain if you invested in common stock. Convertibles are senior securities. In case of default, other bondholders will probably have prior claim on the company's assets. But holders of convertible bonds will have a claim senior to that of stockholders. Furthermore, if there is no default, you will have a guarantee that you will get back at least the face value of the bonds—more, if they are called in before maturity.

You might also be interested in convertibles because you want additional income. The income will not be as great as what you could obtain from a straight bond, but the yield is almost certain to be more than that on the related common stock.

Finally, while enjoying both of the above benefits, you may hope to achieve capital gains. Such gains can be every bit as sizable as those you might achieve by investing in common stock. Indeed, the conversion privilege is the outstanding feature of convertible bonds— the feature that makes them different from and, in some ways, more attractive than regular bonds.

Thus we see more fully why convertible bonds are sometimes termed the ideal investment and said to partake of the best of both worlds. They often prove especially attractive when the stock market's course seems uncertain—when the investor thinks it may go up but wants protection against the possibility that it will go down.

Pitfalls to Convertibles

Are there then no dangers to convertible bonds? There are plenty.

Different investment counselors may give different advice on the purchase of convertibles, depending on their viewpoints, the outlook for the stock market and an investor's individual needs. But on two points, you will find almost universal agreement.

First, be cautious about buying convertibles if safety of principal and liberal income are very important to you. Regular bonds usually are safer and provide more income. In this connection, a key factor to consider is whether the convertible is selling above its investment value and, if so, by how much. The larger the premium is, the less protection you will have against a downward movement in prices.

Second, never buy convertibles unless you have good reason to believe in the soundness of the related stock. A convertible cannot be considered in a vacuum. It must be considered together with the stock. Their fates are inevitably intertwined. If the stock rises in price, so will the bond. If the stock falls in price, the bond will follow suit.

Another danger lies in the fact that convertibles of questionable merit often flood the market. This is especially apt to occur during bull markets, when many second- and third-line companies try to take advantage of investor euphoria by rushing out convertibles.

Then too, even the best convertible bonds are subject

to the same market forces as regular bonds are. If interest rates rise, bond prices will usually fall.

Finally, there is sometimes a danger that a convertible will not be protected against dilution. In other words, the issuing company may split its stock, pay a stock dividend or merge with another company. Against such eventualities, a convertible's indenture will ordinarily require that an appropriate adjustment be made in the conversion ratio. But there have been exceptions to this rule, and these exceptions should be watched for.

There are yet other dangers to convertibles. These will become apparent as we consider what makes a good convertible. When should you consider buying such? And when should you consider converting?

As we have seen, a good convertible has a very sound company behind it. Among other things, this means that the company earns several times the interest it must pay on all its senior securities.

A good convertible also has a sound future ahead of it. In particular, this means that the outlook for its related common stock is bright.

A good convertible offers some protection against a fall in price. In this connection, a convertible selling only, say, 15 percent above its investment value offers considerable protection against a fall in price. A convertible selling for 40 percent or more above its investment value offers only modest protection.

A good convertible also offers a good chance for appreciation in price. The extent of this opportunity will be related, in considerable measure, to the size of the conversion premium. A premium of 50 percent or more is normally considered large.

That means the common stock may be a better buy. In buying the convertible, you may be paying more for the conversion privilege than it is worth, although some good convertibles carry conversion premiums well over 50 percent.

The point is that when a convertible sells for more

than its conversion value, it is apt to increase in price less rapidly than the corresponding stock. The bond cannot keep going upward indefinitely. If and when the stock starts to rise in price, the bond will already be selling for relatively more. So its premium over conversion value will tend to narrow rather than to widen.

One way to help decide whether a conversion premium is too large is to compare the premium with the difference between the yield on the bond and that on the related stock. In doing so, you will determine the number of years the convertible needs to be held to compensate for the possible loss of its premium. Professionals call this the *recoupment period* or simply "break even."

You can make this calculation by subtracting the yield on the related common stock from the yield on the convertible bond and dividing the premium by the resulting figure. For example, suppose the stock yields 4 percent, the bond yields 8 percent and the premium is 20 percent. You would subtract the first percentage from the second, divide the result into 20 and arrive at five years.

Is this good? Says Richard B. Hoey, vice president and chief economist of Warburg Paribas Becker—A. G. Becker: "As a general rule, a recoupment period of under five years is reasonably attractive and one of under three years is very attractive, unless there is a risk that the bond may be called."

You should be aware that a "break even" analysis is simplistic because it disregards taxes and the possibility of a future increase in dividends. Even so, it is one useful way of deciding whether a conversion premium is way out of line.

Finally, and perhaps most important of all, if a bond is selling well above its call price, it may be called in. Then you may lose considerable money.

Take an example. Some years ago, a typewriter manufacturer's convertibles were selling for 125. At that time, their conversion value was about 117. Although this premium over conversion value was not overly worrisome, the bonds had a call price of 106. And when they were suddenly called in, their open-market price quickly tumbled from 125 to 117, which represented their real worth.

The investor then had three choices: He could turn them in at the call price, he could sell them at the new open-market price or he could convert them into stock. Either of the latter two steps was preferable to the first. Even so, if he had purchased ten such bonds at their old market price of 125, he lost about $800 on the sale or conversion.

Nor is this an isolated example. In recent years a number of companies have issued convertible bonds, then called them in. In fact, some have made their calls only a few months after issuing the bonds.

Now let's look at a particular convertible bond in light of the various terms we have just examined. It was recommended recently by Preston Harrington III, an analyst in the fixed-income research department of Merrill Lynch, Pierce, Fenner & Smith.

The bond was issued by Security Pacific, one of the nation's largest banks. It matures in 2006, pays interest of 9.75 percent and is rated AA by Standard & Poor's.

At the time of the recommendation, the bond traded at 79½, 16 points or about 25 percent above its estimated investment value of 63½. Its current yield was 12.26 percent, which is generous for convertibles, and its yield to maturity was 12.46 percent. Both yields were high enough to provide significant defensive strength, Harrington said, and also well over 3 percentage points higher than the yield on the related common stock.

This stock, which Harrington termed attractive, was trading at 27⅝, giving the bond a conversion value of 68.2. With the bond trading at 79½, the conversion premium was about 11 points or 17 percent. Harrington termed this premium reasonable, especially in a period of depressed stock prices.

Each bond is convertible into 24.691 shares of common stock at 40½ a share. The analyst estimated the stock would have to rise in price from about 27 to about 50 before Security Pacific would be apt to call in the bond, which it could do at a price of $109.10.

In sum, said Harrington, "The convertible has a moderate conversion premium, a call on an attractive common stock and a high yield. It also provides strong protection against a decline in price. In fact, the bond should come much closer to matching the price movement of the stock if the stock rises than it is apt to do if the stock falls."

Harrington's only negative: The bond's "break even" or recoupment period worked out to four years, which he termed longish.

We have now applied several tests to convertibles—their market prices in relation to their investment values, conversion values and call prices. It should be obvious that few bonds meet all these tests perfectly. Some compromise is often in order. How much of a compromise should be made depends on your needs and wishes, plus conditions in the market.

Suggests Preston Harrington: "Investors of convertibles who are primarily interested in capital gains should seek bonds with low conversion premiums. Investors who emphasize income and safety of principal should seek bonds with low investment premiums and give only secondary attention to the bonds' conversion premiums."

When to Convert

Once you buy, when, if ever, should you convert? The best answer is: rarely. In fact, only two occasions come quickly to mind. You must convert or sell—or lose money—if the issuer calls in its convertibles when they are selling above their call price. And you may want to convert if you are very interested in good yields and the issuer's stock starts to yield more than its bonds.

Otherwise, there's not much point in converting. If you are seeking capital gains, the bonds usually will be safer than the related stock. After all, you always have the bonds' face value to fall back on. And if you want to sell the bonds and take your profits, you will probably do as well to sell them directly as to convert them, then sell the stock.

The suggestions in this chapter represent basic advice on investing in convertibles. There are more sophisticated techniques available. Often they involve hedging. For example, an investor may buy a convertible and at the same time sell the related stock short—that is, borrow some from his broker, sell it, then plan to buy it back at what he expects will be a lower price.

Techniques like this are often designed to take advantage of price differentials in two or more securities issued by the same company. They not only require expert timing, but also a sophisticated knowledge of the bond market. They are not recommended to the average investor.

What should you remember from this chapter? First, remember that by putting your money in convertibles, you give up some of the safety and some of the income you would receive from regular bonds in exchange for the prospect of above-average capital gains. Second, remember that convertibles often fluctuate in price to a far greater degree than regular bonds do. This may be no great cause for concern if you buy a convertible at or below its face value and plan to hold it until maturity. But it should be cause for considerable concern if you have to sell earlier. Finally, remember at least two of the technical terms in connection with convertibles. One is investment value, the level below which a convertible's price will not usually fall because it represents its estimated worth as a straight bond. The other is conversion value, the convertible's worth in terms of the stock for which it may be exchanged.

6.

Municipal Bonds: The Rich Man's Friends

Next to bonds issued by the United States government or its agencies, municipal bonds are usually considered the safest of all senior securities. That's because they are frequently backed by the full taxing power of the state or city that issues them.

Yet in recent years, the common assumption that municipal bonds are very safe has had to be qualified. There are two closely related reasons why.

There was a day when the municipal bond market was dominated by institutional investors, in particular by commercial banks and insurance companies. Yet, for a variety of reasons, municipal bonds have become less attractive to these institutional investors. And by 1981, according to Salomon Brothers, individual investors were purchasing more than 70 percent of new municipal issues. For the time being this trend is expected to continue.

As the number of individual investors increased over the past decade, some municipal bond dealers began to prey on them. These dealers touted bonds of inferior quality, lied about the true nature of the issuers and misrepresented prices, yields, maturities and heaven knows what else. One popular trick was to refer to certain municipals as "of a quality"—a verbal play upon the A ratings issued by Moody's and Standard & Poor's and a flagrant misrepresentation of the caliber of the bonds.

Despite instances such as this, which cost some investors many thousands of dollars, it would be grossly unfair to imply that the municipal bond market has become rife with corruption. In fact, the unethical dealers have been few in number. But they have received a great deal of publicity, and their existence points up one fact you should never forget if you ever consider purchasing municipal bonds: Be very sure of the reputability of the dealer from whom you make your purchase.

The basic problem is that, unlike the corporate bond market, the municipal bond market is largely unregulated by the United States government, the Securities & Exchange Commission or any other agency. Until recent years this lack of regulation was not considered particularly dangerous because the market was so heavily dominated by institutions, and it was presumed that they could take care of themselves.

There's another reason why municipal bonds *as a group* are not as safe as they once were. Like many corporations, some states and cities have experienced erosion in their creditworthiness and credit ratings. In recent years both Cleveland and New York City temporarily defaulted on loans. And by late 1981 Moody's gave triple-A ratings to only four of the country's twenty largest cities. Furthermore, it awarded ratings of triple-B or lower to a number of cities, such as Detroit, Philadelphia and Pittsburgh. Many institutional investors consider a triple-B rating high enough to warrant investment, but the point is that many cities once had higher ratings.

States have fared better, but even some of them have suffered downgradings. For example, in recent years Standard & Poor's has lowered ratings on debt issued by Minnesota, Oregon and Wisconsin, among other states.

There are many reasons for this state of affairs, including a poor economic climate in some areas of the country and loss of federal aid. But the problem is exacerbated because states and cities need to borrow more money than is available and because the United States government is taking a bigger and bigger share of the credit pie, crowding out other borrowers.

This cloud over municipal financing may or may not have a silver lining, but it does have one good result as far as the investor is concerned. State and local borrowers have recently been paying interest rates equal to 80 to 85 percent of the rates on taxable corporate bonds. Historically, municipal borrowers have paid 65 percent or even less of what corporate borrowers have paid simply because the interest on their bonds is tax-exempt.

Now let's examine municipals themselves. Fortunately, they have many of the same features as corporates. And the few differences between them are much easier to understand than the differences between straight corporates and convertibles.

Municipals are issued not only by cities, but also by towns and villages, by states, possessions and territories and by various public authorities on all these levels of government. The latter include bridge and tunnel, housing, port and other kinds of authorities.

These various bodies issue bonds for all kinds of purposes, but usually do so to finance new construction, ranging from jetports to parking facilities, from public transportation to sports arenas, from waterworks to waste disposal plants. These bodies also seek money in the same way corporations do. They go to an underwriter and entrust him with bringing their bonds to market.

The resulting issues possess almost all of the features that corporate bonds do. In other words, they carry the names of the issuers, bear fixed rates of interest payable over the life of the bonds, are issued at certain initial prices and thereafter trade at whatever prices they can command in the secondary market. They also boast current yields and yields to maturity, and usually they can be called in before they mature.

How, then, do municipals differ from corporates?

First and foremost, the interest from municipals is exempt from taxation. For this reason, the bonds are frequently referred to as tax-exempts. Indeed, the terms "municipals" and "tax-exempts" are used so interchangeably that it is hard to say which is more common.

This exemption is the chief reason why municipal bonds are considered among the most attractive of all investments. Because of it, municipals can carry much lower rates of interest than corporates, although, as noted, the gap is much narrower than it has usually been in the past.

Municipals' tax-exemption means that they are exempt from federal income taxes. Yet they are usually also exempt from income taxes imposed by state and local governments when purchased by individuals living in the states of issue.

For example, if you live in New York State, you probably would not have to pay state or local taxes on any bonds issued by any governmental unit or authority in that state. But you probably would have to pay taxes on bonds issued by or in another state. Since state laws vary somewhat, it's usually wise to check the law in one's own state before purchasing municipals.

The only bonds exempt from all state and local taxes are those issued by Puerto Rico, Guam and the Virgin Islands. These bonds are known as triple-exempts (from federal, state and local taxes). They are very popular.

Why They Are Tax-Exempt

Why are municipal bonds tax-exempt? One reason arises from various rulings made by the United States Supreme Court. As far back as 1819, in a case known as *McCulloch* v. *Maryland*, the court ruled that the United States government could not tax the means or instrumentalities of the various states—and vice versa. As Chief Justice John Marshall saw it, the power to tax was the power to destroy, and his court ruled that neither the federal nor the state governments had the right to tax or destroy the other. The Court has reaffirmed this ruling many times over the years.

There is an additional reason why municipal bonds are tax-exempt. If they were not, they would have to return considerably more interest to attract investors. The interest would have to be paid by taxpayers, thus pushing up property, sales and other local taxes. As a result, many much-needed bond issues would never be voted into existence.

Municipal bonds usually are *serial bonds*. Most corporates, by contrast, are *term bonds*. Serial bonds mature in annual installments. Term bonds mature all at once except, of course, when they are retired periodically by means of sinking fund payments.

The Platte River (Colorado) Power Authority, for example, recently issued more than $34 million worth of municipal bonds in serial form. Some will mature in 1986, some in 1987, some in 1988 and so on right through 1996.

When municipal bonds are brought out in this fashion, either their interest rates or their yields usually rise over the bonds' life. In other words, the bonds with later maturities usually return more than those with earlier maturities.

Why are municipals usually issued in serial form? First, it enables the cost of a civic improvement to be shared among its present and future beneficiaries. Second, it reduces the overall cost. An underwriter can do better by breaking an issue into short-term, medium-term and long-term bonds and pricing each category according to the going interest rates affecting that category.

Issuance of municipals in this fashion is also a boon to investors. They don't have to put their money into bonds that won't mature for twenty or thirty years. They can put it into bonds that will mature in one year or four years or twelve years or whatever period they like. Or they can spread their investment over several maturities so that they can get some of their principal back each year or every few years.

As we have already seen, virtually all municipal bonds issued since the midpoint of 1983 have been registered bonds. Historically, however, most municipals have been bearer or coupon bonds, presumed to belong to whoever possesses them. And there are still thousands upon thousands of municipal bearer bonds around, as there will be for many years to come. So if you ever buy some in the secondary market, keep them in a safety deposit box or otherwise safeguarded. Although thefts may be infrequent, they do occur.

Take what *The New York Times* tagged as The Case of the Albuquerque Eights. In 1970 Albuquerque, New Mexico, issued $9.2 million worth of bonds to finance a convention center. Some of the bonds paid 8 percent interest.

A few weeks after they were issued, a Mrs. Ruth Gitten of New York City purchased $45,000 worth of the bonds from what was then Bache & Co., one of the nation's leading brokerage houses, and is now Prudential-Bache Securities. Bache mailed her the bonds by registered mail.

Unfortunately, they never reached her. They were kept in a safe in a United States post office over a weekend, and somebody broke into the post office and carted off the entire safe. When it was recovered, the bonds were missing.

They turned up in the hands of one Benjamin S. Haggett, Jr., a vice president of the Meadow Brook National Bank in nearby Queens. Haggett pledged the bonds as collateral on a loan from the Republic National Bank of New York. Later he asked Republic National to sell the bonds and pay off the note, which it did. The bonds were then sold from one securities concern to another and finally to the First National Bank in Albuquerque, which happened to be the agent that paid interest on them.

First National discovered that they were stolen when one of its departments tried to obtain interest payments from another department. The bank then traced the bonds back to Republic National and Benjamin Haggett. Nearly a year after the theft, Bache repaid Mrs. Gitten for her loss, and she deposited the money in a savings account. Seventeen months after that, Haggett was sentenced to five years in prison for possessing bonds he knew had been stolen.

As we have seen, most corporates are issued in denominations of $1,000. Most new municipals, on the other hand, are issued in denominations of $5,000. Nonetheless, their prices are still listed as if they had par values of $1,000—that is, at 100 or something above or below that figure.

Yet, if you actually talk to a dealer about municipals, he will refer to most of them in terms of their yield to maturity or, as the trade puts it, on a yield basis. For example, a typical quote might be: state of Louisiana 5½s of 2/01/93 at a 12 basis. This would indicate that these bonds pay 5.50 percent interest, mature on February 1, 1993, and will yield 12 percent if held to maturity.

A reasonable number of corporate bonds are listed on the New York Stock Exchange, the American Stock Exchange or regional stock exchanges. Almost all municipal bonds, by contrast, are traded in the over-the-counter market.

Yet of the thousands upon thousands of separate municipal bond issues available, many are never traded, or are traded only occasionally. That's because many investors tend to purchase them, then hold them until maturity.

Because of the size of the market and the somewhat limited trading in seasoned issues, municipal bond prices are almost never listed in daily newspapers. You can only ascertain their prices by consulting a bond dealer or your stockbroker.

Either one is likely to refer to *The Blue List of Current Municipal Offerings*, a thick, daily publication informally known as the blue list, or *The Blue List Bond Ticker*, an on-line computerized retrieval system that provides the same data that appear in the publication. Both sources list municipal bonds that dealers are trying to sell, plus the bonds' offering prices, yields and so forth.

A dealer may not be able to tell you a bond's rating because a sizable minority of municipal bonds are not rated at all. Although this can be a danger sign, it is not invariably so. A municipality may not have enough debt outstanding to warrant a rating. Or it may not have applied for a rating. Or it may have issued revenue bonds, whose payments of principal and interest are dependent upon the revenue they generate from a particular project, such as a sports arena. The investment advisory organizations occasionally do not rate revenue bonds until the related facilities have had some operating experience.

So much for the differences between municipals and corporates. As you can see, the most important differences are that municipals provide tax-exempt income and are usually issued in serial form.*

---

*Those few municipals issued in term form are known in the trade as *dollar bonds* because they are quoted in terms of their prices rather than their yields.

How Tax-Exempts Vary

Within this broad framework, municipal bonds break into several general categories. These categories reflect the sources of revenue that stand behind the bonds' expected principal and interest payments.

First come *general obligation bonds*. They are backed by the full faith, credit and taxing power of the issuer. In other words, the issuer promises to use its full taxing power to ensure that principal and interest are paid on time.

General obligation bonds have the strongest backing of all municipals. For this reason they tend to receive the highest credit ratings and return the lowest yields.

Generally, holders of these bonds have the first claim on a state's or city's revenues. Yet over the years the question has sometimes arisen whether such bondholders could actually exert this claim in case of default. As the question is often put: Would a city really pay interest to its bondholders before it paid salaries to its policemen and firemen?

Court cases have been extremely limited and the decisions somewhat conflicting. But the question is something of an abstraction. Very few municipal bonds, let alone general obligation bonds, enter default.

Second come *limited-tax, general obligation bonds*. These bonds are identical with general obligations in all but one respect: There is some limit on the taxing power the issuer will exert to pay principal and interest. For example, the issuer may limit the rate at which it will levy property taxes. Or it may set aside only a certain stipulated amount of these taxes.

Third come *special-tax bonds*. These bonds are not secured by the full faith, credit and taxing power of the issuer but by some special tax. For example, they may be secured by a tax on gasoline or a tax on tobacco products.

Fourth come *revenue bonds*. These bonds are secured

only by the earnings of the facility that was constructed from the proceeds from the bonds' sale. This may be an airport, an electric or gas system, a toll bridge, a turnpike or some other facility useful to the general or a specific public.

As a group, revenue bonds are considered less safe than general obligation bonds. This viewpoint is both fair and unfair. Over the years revenue bonds have been in default much more often than general obligation bonds. Even so, their total number of defaults has been small. And some dealers assert that some revenue bonds are superior to some general obligation bonds. So much depends on the revenue generated by a particular facility.

As we learned in Chapter 3, the Chesapeake Bridge and Tunnel Authority's Series C bonds went into default—the facility just didn't attract as many drivers as was expected. Yet similar facilities regularly earn more than they have to pay in interest.

Certain revenue bonds are known as *double-barreled bonds*. This means that they are backed not only by the revenues generated by a particular facility, but also by some other source.

For instance, the New York State Thruway was financed partly from revenue bonds and partly from state-guaranteed bonds. The state promised that if revenues proved insufficient to take care of the interest on both bonds, it would pay the interest on the guaranteed bonds. The revenue bonds would then have first call on the thruway's earnings.

Fifth come *housing authority bonds*. These bonds vary greatly in type. Some are guaranteed by the cities in which the housing authorities' projects are located. Thus they are general obligations of the cities in question. Others are issued by a local public housing authority. But if the rents generated by an authority's projects are insufficient to pay interest, the United States government makes up the difference. Still others are revenue bonds pure and simple.

Obviously, the first two kinds of bonds are considered very safe, almost always receive high credit ratings and pay commensurately lower rates of interest. There is nothing inherently wrong with the straight revenue bonds, but you should be aware of what they are and not be confused merely because the issuer includes the name of its state in its title.

For example, the New York State Housing Finance Agency issues bonds for hospitals, mental institutions and public buildings. Yet its bonds are pure revenue bonds and do not carry the legal backing of New York State.

Finally, there are *industrial revenue* or *industrial development bonds,* which skyrocketed into prominence in the late 1960s. To attract industry, a city or town would float a bond issue and use the proceeds to build a plant or other facility desired by a particular company. The company then took over the facility on a rental basis, and its rental payments were used to pay interest on the bonds.

This kind of deal proved so popular that, in 1968 alone, some $1.6 billion of industrial development bonds were issued. Because the interest was tax-exempt, both the U.S. Treasury and municipalities lost revenue at an alarming rate. So Congress passed the 1968 Revenue and Expenditure Control Act, limiting this kind of bond to very small issues and very special purposes.

Yet it left one important loophole, which involved bonds whose proceeds are largely used to finance pollution-control facilities. Hence the rise of *pollution-control bonds,* of which you may have read a great deal in recent years. These bonds are revenue bonds of a varying nature.

Take a real-life example of how they work. In 1981

Forsyth, Montana, a tiny town of some 2,500 residents, issued $360 million in three-year securities to help finance the pollution-control programs of several privately owned utilities in its area. The securities initially yielded 8.75 percent, about 4 percent less than the utilities would have had to pay if they had issued them in the corporate market rather than have a community do the job for them in the municipal market.

Pollution-control bonds have become immensely popular. The reasons for this popularity should be obvious. The bonds offer decided economic advantages to industry, which rarely earns anything from its antipollution efforts. They also offer decided economic advantages to communities, which obtain cleaner air, rivers or whatever at little cost to themselves. Finally, they offer decided advantages to investors, who get a chance to put their money into something with public value that also provides tax-exempt income.

Just as corporations have come up with innovative kinds of bond issues in recent years, so have states, cities and towns. Although these bonds all fall into one of the categories we have just looked at insofar as the source of their revenues is concerned, in certain other respects they are different from any bonds issued in the past.

Actually, many of the new municipal issues resemble the new corporate issues. For example, states, cities and various authorities of those levels of government have sold zero coupon bonds, put bonds that can be cashed in before maturity at their full face value, bonds with warrants attached that permit purchase of additional bonds at the bonds' par value and floating-rate bonds.

In the late 1970s there was even a spate of minibonds sold directly to the public, without the aid of an investment banker, in denominations of as little as $100, $500 and $1,000. Massachusetts was one such issuer, East Brunswick Township, New Jersey, another. Almost all such issues sold out quickly.

A few years earlier another kind of bond came on the market that has proved particularly appealing to many investors. It's known as a *college bond* and has been issued by a sizable number of colleges, ranging from Harvard and Yale in the East to Southern California and Stanford in the West. Colleges use the proceeds from the sale of these bonds for construction and other purposes.

One reason the bonds are so popular is that many of them are collateralized. The issuer has put aside government bonds, common stocks and other securities that it already owns as a guarantee that it will pay back the principal it owes when the bond issue matures.

More recently, in 1982, Dartmouth took the lead in selling *student-loan bonds*, and a number of other colleges have since followed suit. The proceeds from the sales of such bonds go into funds that provide loans to students at below-market rates. This is particularly important in an era when the federal government is scaling back its financial aid to students.

States, cities and so forth issue tax-exempt notes as well as tax-exempt bonds. In 1982 the gross volume of such notes set an annual record of an estimated $42 billion, approximately 37 percent of the dollar total of new financings.

These notes pay interest, have maturity dates and feature most of the other attributes of corporate bonds. Unfortunately, most are sold in minimum denominations of $25,000.

Now let's turn back to municipal bonds and look more closely at their advantages and disadvantages. As we have seen, their biggest advantage is tax-exempt interest. The greater your income, the more this tax advantage is worth.

For example, let's suppose you are single and have total taxable income of $22,000 a year. You buy a municipal bond that yields 12 percent annually. To get the same after-tax income from a corporate bond, you would have to find one yielding 16.67 percent.

Or suppose you are single and have total taxable income of $35,000, on which, of course, you pay taxes at a much higher rate. You also buy a municipal bond yielding 12 percent. To get the same after-tax income from a corporate bond, you would have to find one yielding 20 percent.

And so on right up the line. If your income is $41,000 a year, you would have to find a corporate bond yielding 21.82 percent to get the same after-tax income you would get from a tax-exempt bond yielding 12 percent. And if your income is $56,000, you would have to find a corporate bond yielding a whopping 24 percent. At present there aren't any bonds available of good quality that yield 20 percent or more.

What if you are married and file joint returns? The same rule applies. The more you earn, the more sense it makes to own municipal bonds.

For example, if your joint taxable income is $28,000 annually, you would have to find a corporate bond returning 16.22 percent to achieve the after-tax income provided by a tax-exempt returning 12 percent. And if your income is $45,000, you would have to find a corporate returning 18.46 percent.

You'll find the relationship between the yields on tax-exempt bonds and the yields on taxable securities clearly spelled out in the table on pages 100 and 101. The differences apply not only to corporate bonds, but also to United States government bonds, savings bank deposits and other kinds of fixed-income investments.

Who Should Buy Municipals

Offhand, it may seem as if municipal bonds were just the thing for you. Yet they may not be. Most investment counselors would argue that if you are married and file joint tax returns, you should at least be in the 26 percent tax bracket before you should even consider municipals. This means you should have a joint taxable income after

Tax Free vs. Taxable Income

This table gives the approximate yields which taxable securities must earn in various income brackets to produce, after tax, yields equal to those on tax-free bonds yielding from 9.00% to 14.00%.

The table is computed on the theory that the taxpayer's highest bracket tax rate is applicable to the entire amount of any increase or decrease in his taxable income* resulting from a switch from taxable to tax-free securities, or vice versa. **Comparison of Taxable & Tax-Free Yields.** To see what a taxable security would have to yield to equal the take-home yield of a tax-free security, find your taxable income and read across. The table is based on federal income tax rates as of the date of this prospectus.

Taxable Income 1983

Joint Return (Thousands of dollars)	Single Return	% Tax Bracket	9%	9.50%	10%	10.50%	11%	11.50%	12%	12.50%	13%	13.50%	14%
			Tax-Free Yield of										
			is Equivalent to a Taxable Yield of										
$20.2-24.6		23%	11.69	12.33	12.99	13.64	14.29	14.94	15.58	16.23	16.88	17.53	18.18
	$15.0-18.2	24%	11.84	12.50	13.16	13.82	14.47	15.13	15.79	16.45	17.11	17.76	18.42
$24.6-29.9		26%	12.16	12.84	13.51	14.19	14.86	15.54	16.22	16.89	17.57	18.24	18.92
	$18.2-23.5	28%	12.50	13.19	13.89	14.58	15.28	15.97	16.67	17.36	18.06	18.75	19.44
$29.9-35.2		30%	12.86	13.57	14.29	15.00	15.71	16.43	17.14	17.86	18.57	19.29	20.00
	$23.5-28.8	32%	13.24	13.97	14.71	15.44	16.18	16.91	17.65	18.38	19.12	19.86	20.59
$35.2-45.8		35%	13.85	14.61	15.38	16.15	16.92	17.69	18.46	19.23	20.00	20.77	21.54
	$28.8-34.1	36%	14.06	14.84	15.63	16.41	17.19	17.96	18.75	19.53	20.31	21.09	21.88
$45.8-60.0	$34.1-41.5	40%	15.00	15.83	16.67	17.50	18.33	19.16	20.00	20.83	21.67	22.50	23.33
$60.0-85.6		44%	16.07	16.96	17.86	18.75	19.64	20.54	21.43	22.32	23.21	24.11	25.00
	$41.5-55.3	45%	16.36	17.27	18.18	19.09	20.00	20.91	21.82	22.73	23.64	24.55	25.45
$85.6-109.4		48%	17.31	18.27	19.23	20.19	21.15	22.12	23.08	24.04	25.00	25.96	26.92
over $109.4	over $55.3	50%	18.00	19.00	20.00	21.00	22.00	23.00	24.00	25.00	26.00	27.00	28.00

Taxable Income 1984 and after

Joint Return (Thousands of dollars)	Single Return	% Tax Bracket	Tax-Free Yield of is Equivalent to a Taxable Yield of										
			9%	9.50%	10%	10.50%	11%	11.50%	12%	12.50%	13%	13.50%	14%
$20.2-24.6		22%	11.54	12.18	12.82	13.46	14.10	14.74	15.38	16.03	16.67	17.31	17.95
	$15.0-18.2	23%	11.69	12.34	12.99	13.64	14.29	14.94	15.58	16.23	16.88	17.53	18.18
$24.6-29.9		25%	12.00	12.67	13.33	14.00	14.67	15.33	16.00	16.67	17.33	18.00	18.67
	$18.2-23.5	26%	12.16	12.84	13.51	14.19	14.86	15.54	16.22	16.89	17.57	18.24	18.92
$29.9-35.2		28%	12.50	13.19	13.89	14.58	15.28	15.97	16.67	17.36	18.06	18.75	19.44
	$23.5-28.8	30%	12.86	13.57	14.29	15.00	15.71	16.43	17.14	17.86	18.57	19.29	20.00
$35.2-45.8		33%	13.43	14.18	14.93	15.67	16.42	17.16	17.91	18.66	19.40	20.15	20.90
	$28.8-34.1	34%	13.64	14.39	15.15	15.91	16.67	17.42	18.18	18.94	19.70	20.45	21.21
$45.8-60.0		38%	14.52	15.32	16.13	16.94	17.74	18.55	19.35	20.16	20.97	21.77	22.58
$60.0-85.6	$34.1-41.5	42%	15.52	16.38	17.24	18.10	18.97	19.83	20.69	21.55	22.41	23.28	24.14
$85.6-109.4	$41.5-55.3	45%	16.36	17.27	18.18	19.09	20.00	20.91	21.82	22.73	23.64	24.55	25.45
	$55.3-81.8	48%	17.31	18.27	19.23	20.19	21.15	22.12	23.08	24.04	25.00	25.96	26.92
$109.4-162.4		49%	17.65	18.63	19.61	20.59	21.57	22.55	23.53	24.51	25.49	26.47	27.45
over $162.4	over $81.8	50%	18.00	19.00	20.00	21.00	22.00	23.00	24.00	25.00	26.00	27.00	28.00

*Based upon net amount subject to Federal income tax after deductions and exemptions, plus zero bracket amount.

© Merrill Lynch, Pierce, Fenner & Smith, Inc.

adjustments and deductions of close to $25,000. Many counselors, in fact, would place the minimum considerably higher, perhaps at the 40 percent level, in which case you should have a joint taxable income of nearly $46,000.

The reason is simple. Unless you are retired or for some other reason are interested only in income, you should seek growth in the value of your investments. The chances of obtaining such growth from municipal bonds are limited. Income from a tax-exempt bond equivalent to a 16 percent return from a taxable bond may sound intriguing until you consider that a prudent investor may obtain that much or more, in capital appreciation and dividends, by investing in common stocks.

This doesn't mean that tax-exempts never provide a chance for capital gains. You can buy such bonds at deep discounts, just as you can buy corporates at deep discounts.

For example, as this is written, Lebenthal & Co., a well-known New York City dealer in municipal bonds, is offering some AAA Chicago bonds that pay 3.75 percent interest and that are due to mature in 1994. The price on the bonds is 48⅜, and they yield 11.90 to maturity. After allowing for the capital gains tax, Lebenthal figures that an investor's total return, in interest and capital gains, will amount to 178 percent.

Of course, this return has to be divided by twelve years, and that means that it amounts to less than 15 percent a year. This is a good return, but even allowing for taxes you may do as well in the stock market. But again you may not. It's a case of betting on a virtually sure thing versus a mere possibility.

As we have seen, the municipal bond market also offers infinite choice. And it is growing all the time. In 1982 alone there was an estimated increase of almost $52 billion in net new municipal financings.

But if you decide to buy municipals, bear these tips in mind:

- Look first at bonds issued by your own state or one of its authorities or municipalities. By buying such bonds, you'll probably avoid state and local taxes.
- Check a bond's marketability before you buy it. Good municipals with good ratings are easily salable. But remember that the municipal bond market is always a buyer's market. The price you get will be determined by the best available bid. And if you are trying to unload $15,000 worth of bonds, the typical dealer will not spend as much time seeking the best bid as he would if you were an institution trying to unload $1.5 million worth. For this reason, Alan W. Leeds, a partner in L. F. Rothschild, Unterberg, Towbin, argues that you should never purchase less than $25,000 worth of any one tax-exempt issue.
- Buy into large issues. When a municipality puts out a really sizable issue, it usually must offer a higher yield than would normally be required to attract investors. So you'll get a higher rate. And if you have to sell the bond before maturity, you'll probably get a better price than you would if you tried to unload a bond from a small issue.
- Make sure that any bond you buy has a legal opinion printed on it or attached to it indicating that the bond is legally valid. These opinions are usually included as a matter of course. A bond without one is not considered a valid delivery.

Historically, the major danger to buying municipals has been that they might decline in market value. This danger has become reality for thousands of bondholders over the past two decades. The next greatest danger has been the possibility of default. Fortunately, the latter danger has not been great.

Even during the Great Depression, less than 2 percent

of average state and local debt was in default at any time. And in most cases, municipal bondholders were paid off within a few years. Permanent losses during the 1929–37 period amounted to well under 1 percent of the average debt outstanding.

The record since World War II has been even better. Defaults have been relatively few. And the overwhelming majority have involved unrated bonds.

Of course, the past is an indicator but not a guarantee of the future. But if you want additional protection, you can now buy insured bonds. Thus some municipal issuers seek insurance against default from one or two highly reputable companies. As a result, Standard & Poor's automatically gives insured bonds AAA ratings, even though they might be worth only an A or a BBB on their own. (Moody's does not take insurance into account when making its ratings.)

What important things have we learned in this chapter? We have learned that municipal bonds are issued by states, cities and public bodies on state and local levels. We have learned that the bonds are sometimes guaranteed by the full legal and taxing power of a state or city. We have learned that the interest from them is exempt from federal taxation and sometimes from state and city taxation as well, making the interest much more valuable than an equivalent amount of interest from corporate bonds and other fixed-income investments. We have learned that the bonds are commonly issued in serial form, making it easy for an investor to get his principal back precisely when he wants it. But we have also learned that the wealthier you are, the more valuable the income from municipal bonds is and that you probably should not invest in them at all unless tax-free income is important to you. Finally, we have learned that fraud has crept into the industry to a small but noticeable degree and that you should be cautious about which municipal bond houses you deal with.

7.

U.S. Treasury Securities: A Plethora of Issues

When people talk about government securities, they are not referring to the savings bonds you may have purchased during World War II or some subsequent period. Rather they are referring to four types of securities periodically issued by the U.S. Treasury. These securities are known as bills, certificates or certificates of indebtedness, notes and bonds.

What are their attractions?

First, they provide maximum safety of principal. In fact, there simply are no safer investments. That's because they are backed by the full faith, authority and taxing power of the United States government itself. If the government ever defaulted on payment of principal or interest, the country would be in very serious condition, both nationally and internationally. Indeed, our entire economic structure would be in jeopardy, and it is likely that many municipal and corporate bonds would also be in arrears.

Second, they are highly liquid. If you have to sell a government security before it matures, you will almost invariably find a ready market for it. And the risk that its price will have fallen substantially below the price you paid for it would be somewhat less than for other kinds of bonds. Among other reasons: The securities are considered even safer than top-rated corporate bonds.

Third, government securities often offer attractive yields to persons interested in current income. Because these securities are the safest of all investments, the yields on them are never quite as high as those on corporate bonds. Even so, the difference is sometimes very narrow.

Ordinarily, the difference ranges from as little as .33 of a point to something over 2 points. The spread tends to widen when investors become unusually concerned about safety of principal, as they did when the Penn Central Railroad went bankrupt some years ago, or when there is an unusually large supply of government issues or an unusually small supply of corporates.

Finally, the interest from government securities is exempt from all state and local income taxes. But it is not exempt from estate and gift taxes imposed at these levels nor from federal income, estate and gift taxes.

Safety of principal. Unusual liquidity. Attractive yields. Limited taxation. These are the chief virtues of government securities. There are still others, as we will see later on. But first let's study the nature of the securities themselves.

First come the Treasury *bills*. Each week the Treasury issues two sets of bills—one maturing in 91 days, the other in 182 days or six months. And each month it issues two other sets—one maturing in nine months, the other in a few days less than one year. All of the issues are designed to provide the government with quick and ready cash.

None pays a stated rate of interest. Rather they are sold, both initially and subsequently, at discounts from their face values. Thus the buyer's yield or rate of return represents the difference between what he pays for a bill and what he receives when he redeems it, plus, of course, the period of time for which it is outstanding.

For example, suppose a $10,000 91-day note were selling for $9,800 or $98 of each $100 of its face value. The rate of return would be determined by dividing the discount by the bill's face value and expressing the resulting percentage (.02) as an annual rate, using a 360-day year. Thus:

$$\frac{100 - 98}{100} \times \frac{360}{91} = 7.91 \text{ percent}$$

This result is known as the *discount rate* and, as you can see, it is based on the bill's face value. Some professionals, however, believe another method of computing the yield is even more valid. This method determines the return on the amount actually invested—$9,800—rather than on the security's face value. It is known as the *coupon-equivalent yield* because it compares the bill's yield with those on coupon—or interest-bearing—securities. In the case above, the coupon-equivalent yield is 8.07 percent, or more than the discount rate.

The yield on Treasury bills is largely determined by the law of supply and demand. The bills are very popular with institutional investors, and usually the yield is fixed by competitive bidding.

Individuals, however, usually bid for the bills on a noncompetitive basis. If you were to do so, you would agree to pay the average price of the bids that the Treasury accepts from institutional investors. This would be much to your advantage, because it would mean that you would be able to obtain at least some of the bills, yet not have to outbid others to get them.

You may buy such bills through a broker or your commercial bank. If you are an important customer, a bank may charge you nothing for the service. If you are not an important customer, it may charge you anywhere from a few dollars to $25 or more, which will, of course, reduce your yield from the bills.

Better yet, when the bills are first issued, you may buy them from one of the nation's twelve Federal Reserve Banks or their thirty-seven branches, either by mail or in person. The Federal Reserve Banks and branches make no charge on either purchase or redemption.

A fact sheet on how to make such purchases—or tenders, as they are known—is available from the banks themselves or from the Bureau of Public Debt, Department of the Treasury, Washington, DC 20226. Basically, all that's involved is writing a certified personal check payable to the Federal Reserve Bank for the full face value of the bond you wish to purchase.

Once the discount rate is established, the Federal Reserve Bank will refund the difference between what you paid and what the bills actually sold for and forward you an ordinary receipt as proof of ownership. It will also make a *book entry* to record your ownership. At one time you could have obtained the actual security, but this has not been possible for several years. When the issue matures, of course, you must redeem the bill or use it toward purchase of a new one.

If you want to buy a bill after its initial issuance or to sell one before its maturity, you can always do so in the active secondary market. But because the bills are outstanding for such short periods of time, there is usually little point in doing so except in an emergency. You will have to pay bank or broker fees, as the Federal Reserve Banks do not maintain a secondary market in the issues.

In addition to being cost-free when they are purchased from a Federal Reserve Bank, the bills possess all of the advantages of government securities cited earlier, plus a rather special one of their own: They are often considered a very good place to put one's money during periods of stock market uncertainty.

If the market seems unstable, you can sit on the

sidelines for a few months until the situation becomes clarified. All the while, you will receive some return on your money. Indeed, reports Henry Kaufman, the famous economist with Salomon Brothers, "In 1981 the simple theory of rolling over, or reinvesting, in three-month Treasury bills as they matured, returned a stunning 15 percent."

It's amusing to note that some years ago the Lady Luck Casino in Las Vegas, Nevada, was reported to have invested all of its employees' profit-sharing fund in Treasury bills. The casino's president explained that investing in stocks represented too much of a gamble. He said he'd rather shoot craps.

Drawbacks of Treasury Bills

Despite all their advantages, Treasury bills also suffer from drawbacks. First and foremost, the yields on them fluctuate frequently and sometimes sharply. This means that they are a much better buy at certain times than at others.

For example, at the end of July 1982 newly issued 91-day bills yielded 10.17 percent on a discount basis. Yet in 1981 the yield on such bills had ranged between 9.90 and 17.05 percent. And in 1980 the spread between the year's high and low yields was even wider.

Because the yield often fluctuates so sharply, it is always wise to compare it with the interest payable on other short-term investments or on savings accounts that can be quickly withdrawn without penalty. Sometimes the bills yield considerably more, sometimes not as much. But when the yield is less, the income is exempt from state and local income taxes, while the interest from other investment vehicles usually is not exempt. This factor may more than make up the difference.

Another disadvantage to Treasury bills is that they

can be purchased only in minimum denominations of $10,000 and further multiples of $5,000. At one time they were available in denominations of $1,000. But some years ago they became so popular that the cost of the paperwork involved in processing small bills became exorbitant. Hence the change.

Treasury *certificates* pay a fixed rate of interest and carry maturities of no more than one year. Ever since 1967, however, the government has refrained from issuing certificates, and none are currently outstanding. The reason: The money can be raised more conveniently by bills.

Treasury *notes* also return a fixed rate of interest, payable semiannually. They carry maturities of not less than one year nor more than ten years. The longer the maturity, the greater the interest usually is.

The notes can be bought for more or less than their face value. So their yields may be more or less than their stated rates of interest. The high on seven-year notes in 1982 was 14.88 percent, more than 4 percentage points above the low.

Like Treasury bills, the notes may be purchased on a noncompetitive basis from Federal Reserve Banks at no charge. Or they can be bought through certain commercial banks or brokerages for a fee.

They come in registered form and possess two distinct advantages over Treasury bills. Because Treasury notes are outstanding for longer periods of time, they normally return more interest. And those with maturities of four years or more are available in denominations as small as $1,000, although those with shorter maturities are ordinarily available only in $5,000 units.

Treasury *bonds* have all the features of other kinds of bonds, such as fixed rates of interest and fixed maturities. They are issued for ten years or more. Some, although not all, are subject to call.

In 1981 the yield on the bellwether 30-year Treasury

bonds reached 15.23 percent. This was more than 3 percentage points above the low.

Government bonds possess all the basic virtues of other government securities. In addition, they are usually available in denominations of as little as $1,000 and come in registered form. Like bills, they can be obtained directly from Federal Reserve Banks when first issued. Or they can be bought from the Office of the Treasurer of the United States, Securities Division, Washington, DC 20226. In either case, there is no charge.

In recent years government securities have traded in the over-the-counter market. But in 1974 the New York Stock Exchange announced that it would list all federal bonds and notes, except foreign series. So now they are traded both places as well as on the American Stock Exchange and at least one regional exchange, although the overwhelming majority of trading is still done in the over-the-counter market.

You learned in Chapter 1 what government listings look like. Only two further points need clarification.

Sometimes a government bond's maturity date is listed in hyphenated fashion—for example, 98-93. This means that the bonds will mature in 1998 but can be called in as early as 1993.

Also, quotations of government bond prices often include percentages that reflect their yields to maturity. These yields include not only the interest that the bonds return but also the capital gains or losses, if any, that will be realized when they mature.

Yields to maturity provide a convenient way of comparing bonds. Yet bonds with identical yields may not be equally good buys. One may be selling at a much greater discount than the other. As a result, a larger part of its yield to maturity will represent potential capital gains. Naturally, this gain will be taxed at a lower rate than the interest.

It is possible to buy government bonds on margin.

Often, in fact, the margin required by brokerage houses does not exceed 10 percent, which is considerably less than that required for corporate bonds and stocks.

As a result, it is very easy to speculate in government bonds. As we saw in Chapter 3, both the potential rewards and risks are very great. But speculation like this is for the hardy with money they can afford to lose. So many factors impinge on the movements of long-term interest rates that it is even difficult for professionals to be sure whether they will rise or fall—and by how much.

There's one other kind of government bond in which you may be interested. Because it's suggestive of funerals, it's known as a *flower bond.*

Flower bonds are usually available at less than their face value because they pay low rates of interest. And if they are in the owners' estates at the time of death, they may be redeemed at their face values to pay estate taxes, no matter what prices they are currently selling at.

The bonds will be valued at their face values to help determine the size of the owners' estate. And these values will, of course, have some effect on the amount of estate taxes due. But there will be no capital gains taxes due on that portion of the bonds' face value used to pay estate taxes.

If these bonds interest you, it's worth mentioning that they will not be around forever. The last new issue came out some years ago. Congress has prohibited the issuance of any more, and those still outstanding are being rapidly retired. In two very recent years alone, the supply contracted 38 percent.

You can obtain a free list of those still available directly from the government. Write the Bureau of the Public Debt, Department of the Treasury, Washington, DC 20226.

Savings Bonds' New Look

Now let's turn to those old favorites—savings bonds. They come in two forms. The better known are called Series EE bonds. The others are known as Series HH bonds. (Until 1980 they were known as Series E and Series H bonds, and some from these two groups are still outstanding.)

Millions of Americans have purchased savings bonds over the years. But, except in time of war, they may not have been wise to do so. Although the bonds are considered very safe investments, the return on them has never been especially good.

This return gradually increased from 2.9 percent in 1941 to only 9 percent in 1981—well below what money market funds were returning in the latter year.

Then, in November 1982, the government made an important change in the program—a change designed to make the bonds more competitive with other short-term investments. Specifically, it stipulated that all new Series EE bonds sold after November 1, 1982, would yield 5.5 percent if held for one year, 6 percent if held for two years, 6.5 percent if held for three years, 7 percent if held for four years, and 7.5 percent if held for five years.

If held for a full five years or more—and this is the change in the program—the bonds will return a variable rate of return equal to 85 percent of the *average* yield on U.S. Treasury securities with five years to maturity. Whatever this rate may be, the government has promised that investors will earn a minimum of 7.5 percent annually. They may, of course, earn more.

There was, of course, no guarantee that the variable rate of return would be high. It could dip well below the old fixed rate of 9 percent that the government used to pay, although not below the 7.5 percent floor cited above. In short, the government has taken away a higher *sure* rate of return—9 percent—and is offering investors a chance to earn even more than 9 percent, with the concomitant risk that they may earn less.

An important note: This risk of a drop in yield below 9 percent applies only to new purchasers of the bonds. Investors who purchased the bonds before November 1982 and continued to hold them thereafter will receive at least 9 percent in annual yield when they cash them in, and even more if the variable rate stays above 9 percent. The same caveat applies to owners of most old outstanding E bonds, the predecessors of EEs. They will receive either the rate they were guaranteed at purchase or the new variable rate, whichever is higher.

The Series EE bonds are sold in eight denominations, ranging from $50 to $10,000. Since the bonds are available at a 50 percent discount from these face values, a $50 bond costs $25, and a $10,000 bond costs $5,000.

No individual may buy more than $30,000 worth (face value) of the bonds in any one year. But two individuals, such as a husband and wife, may jointly purchase $60,000 worth in that period.

The bonds cannot be called in, are available only in registered form, and may be bought or redeemed through the Bureau of Public Debt in Washington. If any bonds you own are lost, stolen or destroyed, the Treasury will replace them without argument. Federal Reserve Banks and their branches, or ordinary commercial banks, will handle redemptions or replacements for you at no charge.

In addition, the bonds are free from income taxes and personal property taxes at the state and local level, although not from other kinds of taxes at these levels nor from federal income, estate or gift taxes. Yet a clever investor may escape taxes altogether—and in very legal fashion.

For example, suppose a father (or mother) wants to establish a college-education fund for one of his children. To this end, he buys a $1,000 bond each year and registers it in the child's name.

The first year, he has the youngster file an income-tax return, reporting the interest that has accrued on the bonds. Because the child is apt to be in a very low income bracket, he will probably not have to pay any income taxes on this interest.

The father keeps a copy of the return. Unless the youngster's income status changes and he earns enough money to be subject to tax or receives unearned (interest) income exceeding $1,000 in any one year, he will not have to file further returns. The initial return will establish proof of the father's intent to establish an education fund. When the bonds mature, the youngster will be able to cash them in tax-free because he has, in effect, been reporting the income from them each year they have been outstanding.

Despite their virtues, EE bonds suffer from drawbacks. The owner cannot sell them, give them away or use them as collateral for a loan. He will obtain the full rate of effective interest only if he holds them for five years or more. And only time will tell how good that rate will be.

Until November 1982, Series HH bonds could be bought over the counter for cash, just like EE bonds. This is no longer the case. Series HH bonds can now be obtained only in exchange for E or EE bonds. More about the merits of such an exchange in a minute.

Series HH bonds are sold in denominations of $500, $1,000, $5,000 and $10,000 and may be obtained from the same sources as EE bonds, at no charge. Unlike EE bonds, however, they are available at their face values, and they return regular interest, which is payable semi-annually.

The amount of this interest rises over the life of the bonds. But if they are held to maturity, ten years later, the interest will average out to 7.5 percent annually. If cashed in early, it will be less.

Series HH bonds enjoy the same basic advantages and suffer from the same basic drawbacks as EE bonds. HH bonds are considered very safe and convenient, are available only in registered form and cannot be called in. Furthermore, they are not subject to state and local income taxes, although they are subject to other taxes at these levels and to income and other taxes at the federal level. On the other hand, they cannot be sold, given away or used as collateral. And the return on them is not as good as that from certain other investments.

But mark this: There is a way to combine the purchase of EE and HH bonds and avoid virtually all federal taxation during one's lifetime. The idea may have particular appeal to people who want to establish retirement funds. It can be implemented as follows:

Over a period of years, buy as many EE bonds as you wish, up to the $30,000 annual maximum. You can defer paying taxes on the interest until you cash the bonds in at maturity.

But don't cash them in. When the bonds mature or within one year thereafter, exchange them for HH bonds worth the same amount. You will not have to pay any taxes on the interest from the EE bonds.

You will, however, have to pay taxes on the interest from the HH bonds. And you will also have to pay taxes on the EE bonds when you cash in the HH bonds or when the latter mature. But these maturities are often extended. So you may end up paying no taxes at all on the EE bonds, in which case they will be taxable only to your estate. (You can follow this same course if you still own old E bonds that have not matured.)

But before exchanging EE bonds for HH bonds, you will want to investigate one possible pitfall. Depending somewhat on how long you held the EE bonds, you may find that the interest from them is greater than it would be from HH bonds. If current income will be very important to you, you ought to weigh this danger carefully.

Until recently, the government also issued U.S. Retirement Plan Bonds, which were available for purchase only in conjunction with bond-purchase plans and pension- and profit-sharing plans set up under the Self-Employed Individuals Tax Retirement Act. Under this Act, qualified individuals could set aside either a portion of their income or a fixed dollar amount yearly, whichever was less, toward retirement. The funds could, of course, be invested in retirement bonds.

But in 1982 the government discontinued sales of such bonds because interest in them had ebbed. Those bought before the discontinuation, however, are still good.

To sum up this chapter, we have learned that the U.S. Treasury issues four kinds of securities—bills, certificates, notes and bonds—plus two kinds of savings bonds. We have learned that all these issues are very popular with investors and are considered as safe as any investment. On the negative side, we have ascertained that although the yields on certain government issues sometimes come very close to matching those on comparable fixed-income securities, they rarely close the gap. In the case of savings bonds in particular, this has proved to be a very serious drawback in the past and may continue to be in the future, although to a more limited degree.

8.

Agency Issues: Uncle Sam's Attractive Nephews

The U.S. Treasury is not the only branch of the federal government that issues bonds and notes. A number of other agencies do, too. Their securities are known as *agency issues* or just as *agencies*.

In recent years the market in these issues has grown remarkably. According to Salomon Brothers, the net increase in privately held federal agency debt amounted to $34.2 billion in 1978. In the ensuing three years there were still further increases, all larger than the 1978 increase. And by spring 1982 this debt totaled $311.1 billion.

The best known of the agencies that issue debt securities for sale to the public are, in alphabetical order:

- The District Banks for Cooperatives, which make short-term and intermediate-term loans to farm cooperatives that market agricultural products.
- The Federal Home Loan Banks, which serve as a reserve credit agency and lender to thousands of savings and loan associations and to other thrift institutions that make mortgage loans to homeowners.

- The Federal Home Loan Mortgage Corporation, often called Freddie Mac, which buys mortgages from Federal Home Loan Banks and other financial institutions and sells them to interested investors.
- The Federal Intermediate Credit Banks, which serve somewhat the same function as the Banks for Cooperatives, lending to various credit associations that in turn make loans to farmers.
- The Federal Land Banks, which are a source of long-term credit to various associations that make loans to farmers to purchase farm machinery, livestock and land.
- The Federal National Mortgage Association, more popularly known as Fannie Mae, which performs various functions in the mortgage market, such as buying mortgages insured and guaranteed by other government agencies, then reselling them to institutions and individuals interested in this kind of investment.
- The Government National Mortgage Association, commonly referred to as Ginnie Mae, which guarantees mortgages that have been issued by banks and other institutions and that have also been endorsed by one or another of various government agencies.
- The Inter-American Development Bank, which makes development loans in Latin and South America.*
- The International Bank for Reconstruction and Development, widely referred to as the World Bank, which makes many of its loans to governments and private organizations in underdeveloped countries.*

It's important to note that in recent years three of these agencies—the Banks for Cooperatives, the Federal

---

*Strictly speaking, these are international organizations, comprised of many nations. But their issues are treated as government agency issues.

Intermediate Credit Banks and the Federal Land Banks—have banded together and sold their bonds collectively. The issues are listed under the name of the Federal Farm Credit Banks.

Most of the issues of these three and the other agencies are much like other bonds and notes. They have face values, pay stated rates of interests and mature on certain stated dates. On the other hand, only occasionally can they be called in ahead of maturity.

We won't examine all of these agency issues. It would be confusing to try to remember all the details. Besides, information about the issues is readily available from most brokers and bond dealers.

How Agency Bonds Compare

Instead we will look in some detail at the issues of the two agencies that are perhaps the most popular of the group. Before doing so, let's see how the agency issues stack up against the various securities issued by the U.S. Treasury.

Agency issues are not considered quite as safe as those issued by the Treasury. The reason: Although a few of the issues carry the full backing of the United States government, most do not. Instead they are backed only by the agencies that issue them. In practice, however, this makes little difference to the safety of the investor's principal. No agency has ever defaulted on its issues.

The United States government would be very embarrassed if one of its agencies did default and probably would take remedial action. Some precedent: During the Great Depression, the Treasury aided the Federal Land Banks when many farmers' mortgages were foreclosed.

But the government usually is not required to render such aid. And for this reason, most agency issues are considered slightly less safe than Treasury issues.

As a result, agency issues almost always return higher yields than Treasury issues. In recent years the difference in yields on issues of comparable maturities has ranged from a few basis points to more than three percentage points, according to Salomon Brothers.

Sometimes, of course, this difference vanishes. But when it rises to a full percentage point or more, the agency issues are usually considered a clearly better buy.

The tax status of the agency issues varies, depending on the agency involved. Ginnie Maes and Fannie Maes are not exempt from state and local income taxes. Yet many other agency issues are, although they are not, of course, exempt from state and local gift and inheritance taxes nor from all the various taxes imposed by the federal government.

To sell their issues, the agencies use fiscal agents in New York City, such as the fiscal agent of the Federal Farm Credit Banks.

When they have an issue to sell, the fiscal agents put together a nationwide sales group and let its members buy the issue at a discount from the listed price. These sales groups usually include banks, brokerage houses and other securities dealers, and the sale of the securities is publicly announced through newspapers and other means.

Each firm that belongs to a sales group accepts orders on the listed terms. If your order is accepted, you will not have to pay a commission. But you may have to pay a service charge, the size of which may vary in accordance with the size of your order. For example, Merrill Lynch, Pierce, Fenner & Smith would charge three eighths of a point for an order for $5,000 worth of agency bonds, one quarter of a point for an order for $10,000 worth, one eighth of a point for $26,000 worth and one sixteenth of a point for an order for $50,000 worth. The brokerage house would actually quote you these charges in thirty-seconds of a point, because that is how government and agency issues are priced.

Only two other special points need to be made about these issues.

First, they come in a wide range of maturities. For example, in 1982 Fannie Mae issued $1 billion worth of debentures due to mature in four years, the Federal Farm Credit Banks $450 million worth of bonds due to mature in eight years, and the World Bank $400 million worth of notes due to mature in ten years. Issues with both shorter and longer maturities are also available.

Second, agency issues also come in a wide range of minimum denominations. Thus many Federal Farm Credit Bank issues are available in units of $1,000. And Ginnie Mae pass-through certificates, which are discussed later on, can be bought only in minimum initial units of $25,000. Yet most other agency issues come in minimum denominations of $5,000 or $10,000, and some agencies put out issues in both sizes.

Let's now turn to the issues of the two government agencies that are, if not the most popular, certainly the best known in the country. The first is Fannie Mae, the second Ginnie Mae.

Fannie Mae performs several important functions, probably the most important of which is the purchase and resale of mortgages insured or guaranteed by the Veterans Administration or certain other government agencies. In connection with its various operations, it issues preferred and common stock, short-term discount notes that are similar to commercial paper, participation certificates that represent shares in obligations held by the Department of Housing and Urban Development and other government agencies plus debentures and notes. For our purposes, the last two are probably of the most immediate interest.

The debentures, which are much like corporate debentures, are issued in widely ranging maturities. The big majority, however, have maturities of no more than ten years, and a number mature in much less time than that, sometimes in only a few months.

None carries the backing of the United States government. Rather they are backed by the cash, mortgages and other holdings of Fannie Mae.

Most of the issues are sold in minimum denominations of $10,000 and further multiples of $5,000. All come in book-entry form only.

The yields on the issues tend to be slightly lower than those on Ginnie Maes but slightly higher than those on Treasury issues. As noted earlier, the income from them is subject to federal income taxes.

In 1968 Ginnie Mae took over some of Fannie Mae's functions. In particular, Ginnie Mae was ordered to make real-estate investment mortgages more attractive to all kinds of investors.

To this end, it backs bonds, participation certificates and *pass-through certificates* that have been endorsed by various government agencies. The bonds are guaranteed by Ginnie Mae itself and often return good rates of interest. The same is true of the participation certificates.

The Most Popular Issue

Yet for a variety of reasons, the pass-throughs are far and away the most popular of the group. They represent shares in pools of mortgages issued by mortgage banks and other institutions and backed by the Federal Housing Administration or the Veterans Administration. Ginnie Mae guarantees *monthly* repayment of both principal and interest, and this guarantee is backed by the full weight of the United States government.

In fact, people who invest in pass-throughs often get their principal back ahead of schedule. This is why the issues are called pass-throughs—repayments above the required level are "passed through" to certificate holders on a prorated basis. Such repayments may come about because of mortgage foreclosures or simple prepayments.

Ordinarily, Ginnie Mae-backed mortgages on single-family units run up to thirty years, those on multifamily units up to forty years. But because the principal is frequently repaid ahead of schedule, the mortgages have an expected average life of twelve years in the first instance, twenty in the second. In short, the owner of a Ginnie Mae pass-through usually can expect to receive his total investment back within twelve to twenty years.

It's important to note, however, that the pattern of repayment has changed in the recent past, particularly on newer issues, and that as a result the average life of thirty-year Ginnie Mae-backed mortgages may not be twelve years, but perhaps fifteen to eighteen years. The actual life of these securities, of course, markedly affects their yields. Thus, if a security is selling for less than its face value and its life is extended, its annual yield will decline.

The certificates are available only in minimum denominations of $25,000 and further increments of $10,000. But the main drawback to them lies in the possibility of early repayment of their principal. After all, when this happens the investor no longer has his investment.

On the other hand, the investor will have obtained a higher yield than he otherwise would have. Furthermore, early repayments can prove a definite advantage in times of rising interest rates. The investor gets his money back and can invest it more profitably elsewhere.

The securities boast other advantages as well. As noted, they carry the full endorsement of the government and are issued only in registered form. They tend to return higher yields than any other government security or agency security. And these yields are enhanced by the fact that interest is paid monthly rather than semiannually.

What is the precise effect of this payment schedule? If, for example, the yield on the pass-throughs is between 13.50 and 13.66 percent, monthly payment of interest will increase the yield another .39 percent on a semi-annual basis. If the yield is between 13.67 and 13.83 percent, the monthly payment will increase the yield .40 percent. And so on up (and down) the line. If the yield reaches 15.28 percent, for example, the addition will amount to .49 percent.

When you get right down to it, Ginnie Maes offer the best features of both mortgages and government bonds. These include attractive yields, unusual safety, easy marketability, and return of principal, although the rate of return has not been as predictable in the recent past as it was in the 1970s.

The securities can be used for a number of purposes— among others, as retirement funds. Indeed, an investor may well receive a higher rate of return than he would from an annuity.

All in all, then, Ginnie Maes may be just the thing for you. At times, however, there may be much to be said for investing in agency issues with terms of five years or even considerably less.

One reason is that in times of climbing interest rates short-term agency issues prove relatively safe. In other words, they are not apt to fall nearly as far in price as long-term corporates and governments are. Also, if you buy short-term agencies when interest rates are not at their highest, you can get your money back as rates begin to rise and invest it elsewhere.

We have learned, then, that a number of government agencies issue bonds, notes and other kinds of securities that are considered almost as safe as those issued by the Treasury itself. We have also learned that these issues come in a wide range of denominations and maturities, tend to return slightly higher yields than Treasury issues do and are very marketable. The main arguments against agency issues are that they do not usually yield as much as corporates and, as a general rule, do not enjoy exemption from federal income taxes, as municipals do. This last drawback, of course, is true of virtually all other non-municipal bonds as well.

As you know, all bond markets have long been dominated by institutional investors. But perhaps nowhere has this been more true than in the market for agency issues. This is too bad, because these issues have something to offer to individual investors interested in bonds. This is not to say that agency issues necessarily should be chosen ahead of corporates, municipals or governments. It is merely to say that investors should be more aware of their availability and merits.

9.

The Mechanics of Buying and Selling Bonds

So far I have said very little about how one goes about buying and selling bonds or about what such purchases and sales cost. To be sure, we have learned that it is possible to buy certain Treasury issues from the Treasury itself or from Federal Reserve Banks at no cost. But these purchases are exceptions to the general rule.

It is important that you know something about the mechanics of buying and selling bonds, because the way you go about making such transactions, and the charges that will be imposed on you, can materially reduce the income or profit you hope to achieve. But before looking at these mechanics, let's grasp three basic points about buying and selling bonds.

First, the cost of buying and selling them is usually much lower than the cost of buying and selling stocks. The reasons for this are varied. For one thing, transactions in bonds usually involve much more money than those in stocks and, as with so many things in life, the more of anything one buys, the cheaper it is apt to be. For another thing, it has historically been easier to execute an order for bonds than it has been to execute an order for stocks. In part, this has been because the great majority of bonds have been issued and kept in bearer rather than registered form, although this trend will now be reversed because the Tax Equity and Fiscal Responsibility Act of 1982 stipulated that, beginning in 1983, almost all new bonds must be registered.

The second point you should understand is the meaning of the term *round lot*. If you have ever invested in common stocks, you know perfectly well what the term means. It means 100 shares of any given stock, regardless of the price at which the stock is selling. Anything less than 100 shares is known as an *odd lot*.

But when applied to bonds, round lot has no such clear-cut definition. In using it while talking to individuals, some bondmen mean five bonds with a face value of $5,000. Others mean twenty-five bonds with a face value of $25,000. Many, perhaps most, however, mean 100 bonds with a face value of $100,000.

However they define round lot, bond dealers all have the same attitude toward it: They would much rather deal in a round lot than an odd lot.

There are three reasons for this. First, in buying and selling bonds, dealers can prosper only by dealing in big volumes. That's because their profits on small transactions are low. Second, if dealers break up round lots to fill orders for odd lots, they may find it difficult to place the leftover bonds. This is particularly apt to be the case if they approach institutions, which are, after all, their biggest and steadiest customers. Third, dealers know that if they fill an order for an odd lot and the customer later wants to sell, he may have to do so at a price several points below the one prevailing in the market. That's because not many other people may want to buy the odd lot. This, of course, will make the customer unhappy and may even cause him to blame his dealer.

From what has been said so far, you may already have guessed the third basic point you should understand. It is not always easy for an individual to place an order for $2,000 or $3,000 or even $5,000 worth of bonds.

Much depends on the individual investment banking firm or brokerage house. Some deal only with institutions. Some do a modest amount of business with individuals. Some do quite a bit of business with individuals, although almost invariably less than they do with institutions.

The First Boston Corp., for one, deals only with institutions. Says one of its executives: "We would handle an order from an individual only in very rare circumstances—if, say, he were the treasurer of a firm that was a very good client of ours. Even then, we would not want to handle an order for five or ten bonds. And if we were willing to handle an order for, say, twenty-five, we would not want to do it very often."

L. F. Rothschild, Unterberg, Towbin, which is heavily, although not exclusively, oriented toward institutions, would ordinarily require a new client to purchase at least five bonds. Other firms, such as Drexel Burnham Lambert, which deals extensively with both institutions and individuals, would impose a minimum charge of $6 a bond for the purchase of only one or two corporate bonds traded on an exchange.

However much business they do with individuals, many firms like L. F. Rothschild, Unterberg, Towbin and Drexel Burnham Lambert do not actively solicit business from customers who want to invest only a few thousand dollars in bonds. And when they are willing to serve such customers, they may do so only after emphasizing the risk involved, in particular the risk that the bonds may be sharply marked down from the prevailing market price if they have to be sold before maturity.

What You Will Pay

How are bonds purchased? As you know, most are sold in the over-the-counter market, which is composed of banks, brokerage houses and other dealers. These various organizations may act either as dealers or as agents.

If they act as dealers, it means that they have underwritten a given bond issue or purchased it for their own inventory. If they act as agents, it means they do not have a given issue in inventory but must purchase it from another dealer.

Obviously, a dealer who has bonds in inventory has incurred some risk. He has assumed that he will be able to sell the bonds at a profit.

The dealer compensates for this risk by trying to build a profit into the price he charges his customers. Thus he will offer you the bond at a *net price* or on a *net basis*. This price will ordinarily include his profit, the profit representing the difference between what he paid for the bond (what's known as the *bid price)* and what he is willing to sell it for (the *ask price).*

Among professionals, this difference is commonly known as a *spread.* You will pay nothing else, except perhaps accrued interest and a postage fee to cover the cost of mailing you the bonds.

The amount of the dealer's spread will vary in accordance with a number of factors, including the nature of the market at any given time, the nature of the firm you are dealing with and the maturity and marketability of the bond you want to buy or sell.

Two other factors will play a role. One is the kind of bond you seek—corporate, municipal, government or agency bond. The other is the bond's age—whether it is a new or a seasoned issue.

The spreads on municipals tend to be the most sizable, those on corporates somewhat less so and those on governments and agencies less yet. Spreads also tend to be somewhat larger on new issues than on seasoned ones.

If the bond were a new municipal, then, as of a recent date, L. F. Rothschild, Unterberg, Towbin's spread usually would have ranged from about $2 to $25, depending on the bond's maturity and rating. If the bond were a new corporate, Drexel Burnham's spread usually would have ranged from about $5 to $10 on orders of $50,000 or more. Spreads on governments and agencies would have been considerably less. As we saw in Chapter 8, Merrill Lynch's spread on a small order would have been only $3.75 per $1,000 bond.

If the issue were seasoned, then the spread would have tended to be smaller, at least on corporates and municipals. In many cases, it would have been about $5 per $1,000 bond, although it could have ranged higher or lower.

All spreads may be quoted in points rather than in dollars. In this connection, an eighth of a point is equal to $1.25, a quarter of a point to $2.50, a half a point to $5, three quarters of a point to $7.50 and a full point to $10.

Although a spread is designed to provide a dealer with a profit, he may suffer a loss instead. For example, suppose a dealer makes a successful bid to underwrite a bond issue at its face value (100) and plans to reoffer it to the public at 100.75. This would give him a spread of three quarters of a point or $7.50 on each bond.

But suppose the issue doesn't sell out. Suppose some remains in his inventory. Suppose interest rates go up, pushing the price of older bonds down. People may no longer be willing to buy his bonds at 100.75 or even 100. He may have to sell them at a loss, assuming he can sell them at all.

If a dealer does not own the bonds you seek, he must act as an agent, in which case he will probably buy them from another dealer. The other dealer will give him a concession—perhaps $2.50 a bond—which will represent the first dealer's profit. In other words, L. F. Rothschild, Unterberg, Towbin at least will charge only what you would have to pay the other dealer if you had bought directly from him.

As we have seen, not all bonds are traded in the over-the-counter market. Some are traded on various national or regional exchanges. If you purchase such bonds, their prices will be determined at auction. And you will pay a commission, usually ranging from $2.50 to $10 a bond.

If and when you want to sell your bonds, the dealer will again impose a spread or charge a commission. If the bonds are corporates or municipals, and if you want to sell a reasonable number of them—say, 25—the spread may often be half a point or $5 a bond. But if the bonds aren't very marketable—liquid, as bondsmen sometimes say—and if you have only two or three of them, the spread may range up to five points or $50.

Cutting Your Costs

Enough of spreads and commissions. What you should remember is that they are normally much less than they would be on stocks, that they vary according to the nature of the bond and the condition of the bond market and that they also vary according to the dealer you are working with. According to Alan W. Leeds, a partner of L. F. Rothschild, Unterberg, Towbin, "I think you will find there is considerable diversity in the spreads on the purchase and sale of bonds."

In other words, it may pay to shop. This can be particularly important in the case of municipal bonds. Some less reputable houses have been known to impose spreads two or three times as big as the average.

How else do you keep your costs down?

Deal only with a very reputable house. Some people in the investment banking business are not nearly as knowledgeable about bonds as they are about stocks. But if they work for a well-regarded house that does any business at all in bonds, it will have a research department on which they can rely for information and guidance.

Don't tie your decision on where you buy solely to the amount of the spread or commission involved. As we have seen, costs can vary. But your main objective should be to buy bonds of good quality.

Have your dealer compute the yield to maturity after all costs have been added. Ordinarily, the price and yield to maturity he quotes you will reflect his spread. But if there are extra costs, be sure the yield to maturity reflects them, too.

The actual placing of an order for bonds with a dealer is little different from placing an order to buy or sell stock. Ordinarily, you can buy a bond by telephone. You can often sell it the same way, although some dealers like to see bonds they sell before making transactions. They say some customers describe their bonds incorrectly over the telephone.

A final word about margins: The New York Stock Exchange currently requires that stocks be bought at no less than 50 percent margin—you must put up at least that much of the purchase price. The margin requirements for bonds are as follows: for corporates, 25 percent of market value for convertibles, 50 percent of market value; for municipals, 25 percent of market value or 15 percent of face value, whichever is less; and for governments and agencies, 5 percent of face value.

Some brokerage houses may require still higher margins. But they cannot permit lower ones.

As we have seen, you can speculate by buying on margin. But these days, it's an expensive proposition, quite aside from the risk involved. Typically, a brokerage house will charge you the broker loan rate, which, while usually less than the prime rate, can be expensive.

If you do margin, be careful not to margin up to the hilt. Leave yourself a little room for a possible drop in bond prices. That way you won't have to put up extra money at a time when it may be very inconvenient.

So much for the mechanics of buying and selling

bonds. As you can see, costs are relatively low. But they can prove expensive if you buy only one or two bonds that are not widely marketable. Furthermore, you may have to hunt a bit to find a dealer willing to handle a small order.

Is there no way that an investor with only $1,000 to put up can buy bonds easily and inexpensively? Yes, there is. He can buy into a bond fund, and that is the subject of the next chapter.

10.

Bond Funds: Are They Worth the Candle?

If you follow financial news, you have undoubtedly heard or read a great deal about bond funds. Actually, they are nothing new. The well-known Keystone Massachusetts funds date to 1932, and several others came into existence within the next decade.

But the great boom in bond funds began during the 1970s, as investors despaired of the stock market and sought refuge in bonds. Indeed, so many funds have come into existence in the past decade or so that it is difficult to ascertain their exact number. Even so, they total in the hundreds.

These funds have proliferated not only in great numbers, but also in great variety. To understand them properly, we must categorize them in three different ways.

First, they must be categorized by their sales charge or lack thereof—whether they are *load funds* that levy sales charges on initial purchases, *no-load funds* that levy no such charges, or *closed-end funds* that are sold on commission like common stocks. Second, they must be

categorized according to their form of organization—
whether they are *open-end (mutual) funds, closed-end
funds* or *unit trusts*. Finally, they must be categorized by
the nature of their holdings—whether they invest exclusively or primarily in corporate bonds, convertible
bonds, municipal bonds or other kinds of debt securities.

In categorizing bond funds, it is important to avoid a
mistake sometimes made in the popular press. We must
not lump bond funds together with income funds nor
refer to the two kinds of funds as if they were the same
thing.

Although they are similar in some respects, they also
differ. Bond funds usually invest all or most of their
assets in bonds. Income funds may put a good share of
their assets in bonds but sometimes invest a majority of
their assets in conservative preferred and common
stocks.

I do not point this out to denigrate income funds,
some of which have proved to be sound investments, but
to remind you that you should always know exactly
what you are buying. In theory at least, income funds
are riskier than bond funds. Yet the former also provide
more potential for capital gains.

Now let's look more closely at the various categories
of bond funds. Bear in mind that all such funds fit not
just one, but all three of the categories listed above. For
example, a fund may be an open-end load fund specializing in corporate bonds. Or it may be a unit trust,
which also charges a load, specializing in municipal
bonds.

Load funds levy an initial sales charge. In some cases,
this charge will run to 8.75 percent of the initial investment, which is comparable to what many mutual stock
funds charge. Yet plenty of such funds charge only 4.5 or
3.5 percent, and at least one charges only 1.5 percent.

No-load funds do not levy an initial sales charge. This

is because they sell their shares directly to the public rather than through salesmen or brokers. Some load funds say the no-load funds don't provide as much service either, but that may be part of their sales pitch.

Like no-load funds, closed-end funds do not levy a sales charge. But you must pay commissions to buy and sell them, just as you would if you were buying and selling stocks.

Whether or not they levy a load, some funds are organized as open-end or mutual funds. Three features distinguish such funds. One, they continually offer new shares to the public and buy back those shares the public wishes to sell. Two, the shares may always be purchased or sold at their net asset value, which is determined by dividing a fund's total net assets by its total number of shares outstanding. Three, the funds regularly buy bonds they consider desirable and sell those they consider undesirable. In short, they seek to increase the overall values of their portfolios as well as return good incomes.

Closed-end funds do not continually offer new shares to the public nor buy back those shares. Once they have made their initial offerings, their shares must be bought and sold in the over-the-counter market, just as individual bonds and stocks are. Furthermore, these shares may be available at either a discount from or a premium over their net asset values or real worth. Often they sell at discounts. Like the open-end funds, however, the closed-end funds ordinarily do buy and sell bonds from time to time.

Most unit trusts invest in municipal bonds and are commonly sold in individual units worth a certain minimum amount in terms of the face value of their holdings. Almost always this minimum is either $1,000 or $5,000, plus a load, plus accrued interest. For example, a municipal investment unit trust recently sponsored by Merrill Lynch, Pierce, Fenner & Smith, Prudential-Bache Securities, Dean Witter Reynolds and Shearson/American Express contains bonds with a total face value of $50 million and is divided into 50,000 units. As a result, the initial offering price, which included a 3.5 percent load and accrued interest, was $1,040.78.

It may seem as if the initial offering price should have been $1,035. The reason it was not is that most bonds in the trust were purchased for more than their face value. The 3.5 percent load was then applied to this premium, rather than the face, value.

Once a trust like this is sold out, a new investor cannot buy into the trust unless some other investor sells his units back to the trust's sponsors, which usually maintain secondary markets in the units. If the funds don't maintain such markets, owners can redeem their units only through the funds' sponsors.

Even though unit trusts limit their membership, new ones are continually being brought to market. In 1981 alone, Merrill Lynch brought out 170 unit trusts, often in conjunction with other firms, such as those cited above. So if you can't buy into one trust, you can almost certainly buy into another.

One of the principal features of these trusts is that they are not allowed to trade bonds. They may sell the bonds in their portfolios only if the bonds go into default or suffer other setbacks clearly detrimental to the trusts' owners.

Also, unlike open-end and closed-end funds, which go on forever, unit trusts have definite terms or lives. The length of their lives varies greatly.

All these different kinds of bond funds differ from one another in one other important respect: They may or may not require an initial purchase of a certain minimum size. Very few impose no minimums. Some require minimums of only $100 or $250. Many, however, insist on minimums of $1,000 or $5,000. Sometimes subsequent purchases may be far smaller.

Now let's look at the funds in accordance with the nature of their holdings.

Corporate Bond Funds

Obviously, these funds invest all or most of their assets in corporate bonds. As you know, such bonds tend to yield more than other bonds, except perhaps for municipal bonds, whose tax-exempt status puts them in a special category.

It's important to understand, however, that corporate bond funds vary greatly. The kind of bonds one fund invests in may be different from the kind another does.

No better example exists than the three Keystone Massachusetts bond funds.* All are open-end load funds specializing in corporate bonds. They are known as B-1, B-2 and B-4.

The B-1 fund is the most conservative of the Keystone Massachusetts group. Ordinarily, it keeps a portion of its assets in bonds issued by the United States government and its agencies or bonds rated AAA, almost all of the rest in bonds rated AA or A. Its annualized yield as of late July 1982 was 11.81 percent.

The B-2 fund is less conservative and invests primarily in bonds rated A or BBB. Its annualized yield as of the above period was 11.31 percent.

The B-4 fund invests almost exclusively in discount bonds, including some rated BBB and some with lower ratings. Because of the comparatively low ratings of many of its holdings, it enjoys or suffers from much

---

*Although I mention certain funds by name in this chapter, this does not constitute an endorsement of them nor a rejection of those not named. I have named certain funds either because they are very well known or because they are reasonably representative of a certain category of funds. You can learn the names and records of other funds by checking various reports, such as *Investment Companies*, put out by Wiesenberger Services, Inc. These reports are commonly available in brokers' offices and public libraries.

wider fluctuations in its net asset value than B-1 or B-2. In short, although it is riskier than B-1 or B-2, it tends to provide a better yield and a better chance of capital appreciation. Its annualized yield, as of the period cited, was 12.06 percent.

Some organizations offer *corporate unit trusts*. These are markedly like municipal unit trusts, which are discussed in great detail later in this chapter. The chief difference between the two kinds of trusts is that the income from the corporate trusts is taxable.

Convertible Bond Funds

These funds, of course, invest most of their assets in convertible bonds and convertible preferred stocks, which, like the bonds, can be converted into common stock. As we saw in Chapter 5, convertibles tend to return less income than most other kinds of bonds. But they also provide much more chance for capital gains.

One of the best known of such funds is the American General Harbor Fund. This open-end, load fund has been in existence since 1956.

As a matter of policy, it seeks to keep more than 50 percent of its assets, exclusive of cash, cash equivalents and government securities, invested in convertible securities. As a matter of practice, it often keeps far more there.

For many of its participants, the fund has done well. For example, if you had invested $10,000 in it at the beginning of 1972, reinvested the dividends you received in the ensuing ten-year period and taken all capital gains distributions in further shares of the fund, your holdings would have been worth about $22,280 by the end of 1981.

But the roller coaster can go down as well as up. If you had invested $10,000 at the beginning of 1981, your investment would have declined in value to about

$8,680 by the end of that year. This is a decline of more than 13 percent, although it is only fair to add that the fund then rebounded about 15.75 percent in the first eight and one half months of 1982.

How about yield? Over the twelve-month period ending in mid-September 1982, it was 6.4 percent.

Municipal Bond Funds

There are a raft of these funds. Merrill Lynch, Pierce, Fenner & Smith and John Nuveen & Co. are the leaders in the field. But a number of other brokerage houses sponsor such funds, too, sometimes jointly, sometimes individually. A partial list of such houses includes Prudential-Bache Securities, E. F. Hutton, Paine Webber, Jackson & Curtis and Dean Witter Reynolds.

Often, municipal bond funds are *municipal unit trusts* sold on a load basis. The load is usually either 3.5 or 4.5 percent of the initial purchase order, depending on the trust.

An investor buys one or more fixed units from such a trust, whose holdings are firmly fixed from the start. Over the years, of course, the trusts will gradually shrink in size as the bonds they own are called in or mature and their owners receive their prorated share of the return of principal. These trusts usually pay interest monthly rather than semiannually.

When first conceived it was believed the trusts would attract small investors. That's because they usually require minimum investments of only $1,000 or $5,000. But they have proved almost as popular with larger investors.

In addition to these trusts, you may run across a special kind of municipal bond unit trust that invests only in bonds issued by a particular state or its cities or various public authorities. Obviously, these funds appeal especially to residents of the state in question.

That's because the income the residents receive from the funds is normally exempt from all federal, state and local income taxes. Residents of other states usually will not have their income from the funds exempted from the taxes imposed by and in their own states. Among other states, some municipal unit trusts are invested solely in securities issued by or in California, Michigan, Minnesota, New York and Pennsylvania.

The state trusts have tended to yield slightly less than general municipal bond unit trusts. On the other hand, the added tax exemptions often more than make up the difference in yields.

Floating-rate municipal unit trusts constitute a recent innovation among municipal bond funds. For the most part, they are very similar to standard municipal unit trusts. The chief difference is that the rate of interest returned by the new trusts floats upward and downward each month in keeping with current market rates.

The disadvantage of this, of course, lies in the fact that the investor can never be sure how much monthly income he will receive. Against this, he will be sure that the market value of the individual units he owns—that is, the capital he invested—will remain stable within a very narrow range. This is not the case with regular municipal unit trusts, where market value will decline when interest rates rise.

Another recent innovation in this field is the *zero coupon unit trust*. These trusts have the same advantages and disadvantages as zero coupon bonds, which were discussed in an earlier chapter.

In addition to municipal unit trusts, there are municipal bond funds. Some are load funds, some are not. But unlike the trusts, they are open-end funds that continually sell new shares to the public. Also unlike the trusts, they are managed, meaning that they often buy new bonds and sell those already in their portfolios. Thus they may achieve capital gains—or suffer capital losses. Again unlike the trusts, they return fluctuating rates of interest.

Which are better—the trusts or the funds? Before buying either one, see how the trusts compare with the funds at a given time and how a particular fund has done for twelve or more months in the immediate past.

Beyond this, keep in mind the following advice from Frank P. Wendt, chairman of John Nuveen & Co., which sells both trusts and a fund. He says: "Which is best often depends on your objective. If you're young and want to build a nest egg, have only $1,000 or so to invest but can reinvest the interest, a fund may be best. If you're older, particularly if you're nearing retirement, a trust may be better because you will be assured of a fixed rate of return."

Government Bond Funds

There are also government bond funds and government unit trusts, both of which invest in securities issued by the U.S. Treasury and in some cases in those put out by various federal agencies. Neither kind of fund should be confused with government money market funds, which are discussed in the next section of this chapter.

Two government bond funds have recently been launched by John Hancock and Kemper. Both are open-end funds whose net asset value may change daily. In addition, both are load funds. John Hancock levies an initial sales fee of 8 percent, while Kemper charges 4 percent.

Both funds invest primarily in intermediate-term issues. The John Hancock fund limits itself to U.S. Treasury issues, and these issues recently had an average life of under five years. At that time the fund yielded 10.21 percent. Kemper invests in agency as well as Treasury issues, and its portfolio recently had an average life of about ten years. Its yield then was 13.14 percent.

There are many other well-regarded government funds around. And from time to time newspapers feature advertisements for government unit trusts. Merrill Lynch, among others, has been a sponsor.

Money Market Funds

Money market funds have been one of the great success stories of the 1970s and early 1980s. These funds got their start very early in the past decade and became popular rather quickly. By late 1982 there were some 275 of them commanding some $230 billion in assets. For millions of Americans, the funds serve as a kind of super savings account. This is because of the very high yields they have usually returned—yields that can, nonetheless, decline quickly and sharply.

The funds invest in so-called money market instruments that usually mature within one year and often within a few weeks or months. These instruments include United States government or agency securities, bank certificates of deposit, banker's acceptances, commercial paper and the like.

The kicker is that the funds are able to invest in certain instruments that are beyond the reach of the typical investor. For example, they can buy commercial paper, which cannot be purchased in units of less than $100,000.

All of the funds are open-end, no-load funds in which you can usually make an initial investment of only $1,000 or in some cases $5,000. Subsequent investments usually can be much smaller.

None of these funds seek capital gains. All are interested only in current income, which most investors simply reinvest.

All in all, money market funds have been extremely successful. The only major argument against them, aside from the fact that sometimes you can obtain higher yields elsewhere, is that they are not insured as bank deposits are nor as the new, bank-sponsored money market plans are. Actually, this risk is more theoretical than real. In all the years they have been in existence, there has been only one case in which investors lost part of their principal, plus one other where they would have lost some principal if the fund's sponsors had not absorbed the loss. Neither of these situations had anything to do with the creditworthiness of the borrowers in whose instruments in the funds had invested. Besides, many of the funds are considering obtaining insurance, which would be attractive to some investors, although it would also reduce the funds' yields.

Significantly, there has been a tremendous boom in money market funds that invest only in U.S. Treasury issues. In the first six months of 1982 alone, about twenty-five such funds sprang up, more than doubling the number in existence at that time. Capital Preservation, Dreyfus, Merrill Lynch and Scudder are among the well-known firms that sponsor such funds.

The disadvantage to the government money market funds is that they return less income than regular money market funds. Over a year's time, the difference may range from less than 1 percent to more than 2 percent. The advantage to the government funds, as well as to the new bank-sponsored plans, is that they may allow some investors to sleep a little more soundly at night.

The Basic Advantages

There are a great many bond or equivalent funds, and they come in considerable variety. Whatever their precise nature, all possess certain inherent advantages in common. Among others:

- *Diversification.* Diversifying one's holdings is almost

always a sound investment principle. Yet, in the case of bonds, it's not always easy to apply. They cost so much that the small investor may not be able to afford more than two or three of them. Obviously, bond funds provide a way around this impasse. And the diversification they offer is sometimes vertical as well as horizontal. As James M. Benham, chairman of the two Capital Preservation funds, puts it: "Many attractive bonds and money market instruments that provide higher than average yields are available only in denominations of $10,000, $25,000 or even $100,000. This puts them beyond the reach of all but the wealthy. But it does not put them beyond the reach of people who invest in bond funds."

- *Professional management.* "This can be even more important in bonds than in stocks," says Michael Lipper, president of Lipper Analytical Services, which keeps track of all kinds of funds. "That's because there is less room for error. Bond prices are largely tied to supply and demand, which in turn are tied to interest rates and the creditworthiness of bond issuers."
- *Relative safety.* Few funds invest in bonds with ratings lower than BBB. Many have the majority of their holdings in bonds or other debt securities rated AAA, AA or A.
- *Marketability.* Except in the case of closed-end funds, you can almost always sell a fund's shares back to its sponsor. This doesn't necessarily provide protection against diminution in net asset value. But it does guarantee that you will be able to unload your shares if and when you want to.
- *Convenience.* If you buy into a fund, you won't have to watch for bonds that are called in before maturity. You won't have to hold onto your bonds or safeguard them. You won't have to clip coupons and

turn them in for payment. The funds will do all these things for you and mail you checks semiannually, quarterly or often monthly.

- *Two-way protection.* Many people who have invested in bonds or bond funds in recent years would have invested in stocks if the stock market hadn't performed in such lackluster fashion throughout much, although far from all, of this period. Yet some funds encourage investors to buy into bond funds, then allow them to invest their interest payments and capital distributions, if any, in stock funds run by the same companies. By following this procedure, investors gain considerable protection for their original investments, yet enjoy a chance to reinvest their interest with an eye to better capital gains than the bond market normally can provide.

All of these advantages are worth pondering. Yet some are not as important as they seem. For example, diversification is probably less important to a bondholder than to a stockholder. That's because the former can achieve maximum safety by buying only top-rated bonds. In fact, he can achieve even more safety than some of the funds promise. That's because they often buy bonds with less than triple-A ratings.

Bond funds suffer from other disadvantages as well. A person who buys bonds directly can pick those with the exact maturities he wants. A person who invests in bond funds can't always do this.

Also, not all of the load funds scale down their sales charges for large investors. The person who buys $100,000 worth of shares may pay just as much, relatively speaking, as the person who buys $1,000 or $5,000.

Even when this is not the case, the cost of buying into some load funds eats heavily into the first year's returns. The investor has to hold onto his shares for several years to amortize its sales charge to any reasonable degree.

What's more, the investor may achieve a higher yield by investing on his own. Even Frank P. Wendt, chairman of John Nuveen & Co., concedes that an investor may gain as much as a percentage point more yield by making his own purchases.

These, then, are the major advantages and disadvantages of bond funds. On balance, how do they stack up? Are they worth the candle?

"Yes," says Henry Kaufman, managing director of Salomon Brothers and one of the most respected economists in the country. "Bond funds provide a way for the individual to participate in the bond market without having to shop around for individual issues, and they are convenient for other reasons as well. Nonetheless, any investor should carefully study the prospectus of any particular fund to find out the degree of diversification he will get and the quality of the investment the fund will make."

And there is the nub of it. Bond funds do deserve consideration. But like any other investment, they also demand caution and investigation. What exactly should you look for?

Certainly, you should look at the nature of any given fund in terms of your own desires and needs. Is it a load fund or a no-load fund? Is it an open-end fund, closed-end fund or unit trust? Does it specialize in corporate bonds, municipal bonds or some other kind of debt security?

How does its nature affect its return? For example, if it's a load fund, by how much will its sales charge reduce your yield if this charge is spread over, say, three years? If it's a government fund, how much lower is its yield likely to be than that from a corporate fund?

Also check the quality of its holdings. Be wary of funds containing a lot of bonds rated lower than BBB. This doesn't mean that funds that own only bonds rated BBB or better are totally safe. It merely means that BBB should be the minimum rating you should expect, unless you deliberately decide to invest in a more speculative fund like Keystone's B-4.

In addition, check a fund's maximum turnover rate, unless, of course, it is a unit trust. A turnover rate of 100 percent means that the fund's entire portfolio may be replaced within a year. A turnover rate of 300 percent means the entire portfolio may be replaced three times a year. As we have seen, there are both advantages and disadvantages to high turnover rates. What is important is that you understand and accept any given fund's policy on trading.

Check, too, a fund's total expenses. The lower they are, the more will be left to pay shareholders. Ordinarily, these expenses do not exceed 1.5 percent of the annual average net assets and often are considerably less.

In short, bond funds merit consideration. But before you buy into one, learn what kind of fund it is. Ascertain what its past record has been. And recognize that, in the world of investments, there is rarely a sure thing.

11.

A Few Words of Advice

Scattered through these pages have been various bits of advice designed to help you evaluate different kinds of bonds and buy and sell them to maximum advantage. Now let's recapitulate the most important parts of this advice and add some further pointers.

All these pointers are merely suggestions. They are probably valid for most people most of the time. But don't hesitate to disregard them if they do not apply to your circumstances in any given instance.

What to Do
First a few do's:

Deal with brokerage houses that have big bond departments. Because they maintain large and varied inventories of bonds, these houses usually can get a better deal for you than most small houses can.

Also, the large houses are more apt to have sizable research staffs. These staffs will be of great aid to your broker if he is not as familiar with bonds as he is with stocks. In fact, some houses require their brokers to consult with their bond department before selling bonds to individuals.

You may also want to check with your bank, especially if it is among the nation's biggest. Big banks often maintain sizable bond inventories and conceivably may do even better by you than a brokerage house will.

In fact, it is wise to shop around among several sources before buying bonds. This can be particularly important if a brokerage house or other dealer is a market-maker—that is, if it buys and sells certain securities for its own account and maintains an inventory in them. You may or may not do better elsewhere. All the same, don't be so concerned over the spread or commission you have to pay that you disregard all other factors, such as the kind of organization you are dealing with, the nature of the bond you are considering, its rating and so forth.

Buy with definite goals in mind. There's no point in investing in bonds or anything else without knowing precisely what your aim is and how to best achieve it.

Are you seeking capital gains? There's nothing necessarily wrong with investing in bonds with this aim in mind, provided you remember that they are not ordinarily considered the best means of achieving capital gains.

Are you seeking income? How much do you require, and for what purpose will you use it? When will you need your principal back?

Narrowing your goals will help both you and your broker decide on the right kind of bonds for you. For example, if you will need your principal back in ten years, then you can limit your selection to bonds that will mature in ten years.

In this connection, you should be aware that, by and large, it is much easier to choose among bonds than among stocks. Even if you limit your choice by several criteria—kind of bond, rating, yield, maturity and so forth—you usually will find a number of different issues that will meet your needs. But it's important to establish these criteria before you start buying.

Buy bonds that are clearly marketable—those that you can sell easily and at a decent price should the need arise. You don't know what the future will hold.

To assure yourself of marketability, avoid bonds from issues of less than $50 million. If you want to do even more to assure marketability, confine yourself to bonds rated AAA or AA or to government or agency issues. Finally, consider limiting your choice to bonds listed on a major exchange. They are more apt to be marketable in small amounts than bonds sold over the counter, although this does not hold true, of course, for municipals, almost all of which are sold in that fashion.

If you want to buy municipals, give serious consideration to buying those issued by or in your own state. This advice is particularly appropriate if you live in a large, heavily populated state that is likely to have many different bonds outstanding. By buying such bonds you will avoid all state and local income taxes and thus increase your yield.

This does not necessarily mean that you should confine yourself to bonds issued in your own state. After all, diversification usually is a sound principle to follow.

Buy new bonds. Some dealers insist that you will do better to buy seasoned issues, and in some cases they may be right. But there is at least one clear-cut advantage to buying new issues: More time will have to elapse before they become subject to call. Therefore, you will be sure of earning interest for a longer period of time.

Review your portfolio annually, whatever its composition. Circumstances change. You may be single one year, married the next, or married, then widowed. You may have a new child, a new home or a new job. Even if your life has undergone no changes, review your portfolio every year. New developments may affect your bonds or the bond market in general. It's true that bonds are usually bought for the long term; even so, never consider yourself irretrievably wedded to a particular security.

What to Avoid

And now for a few don'ts:

Avoid bonds that will be subject to wide fluctuations in price. Obviously, this should not be a hard-and-fast rule. In fact, you probably won't be able to observe it at all if you invest in convertible bonds.

But if there's any chance at all that you will have to sell your bonds before they mature, you must give this rule some weight. Aside from convertibles, the bonds most apt to fluctuate in price are those that will mature well in the future, those that offer yields higher than the going rate right from the start and those that carry low rates of interest.

Obviously, if you apply this rule, you may have to give up one advantage—say, a yield higher than the going rate—to obtain another advantage—price stability. So, more than most, this factor should be weighed together with others, not considered by itself.

Avoid bonds subject to early call, especially if they carry high rates of interest. Otherwise, you may own your investment only a relatively short period of time.

Avoid bonds that are selling for more than their call prices. If they should be called in, you could suffer a loss of capital.

Avoid bonds that have been issued by new companies. Such companies have no track records and for that reason their bonds may be unrated. Even if this is not the case, you'll do well to stick to bonds issued by companies that have been in business a number of years.

Avoid delaying your investment until you think interest rates have hit their peak. This doesn't mean you should give no consideration to rising interest rates. But trying to buy bonds when interest rates are at their crest is like trying to buy or sell a stock when it hits its bottom or reaches its top. Few people are able to pick the exact day when stock prices hit their lows or highs—or when interest rates reach their zenith.

Avoid bonds with low ratings unless you definitely want to speculate. This means you should not buy bonds with ratings of less than triple-B. And if safety of principal is extremely important to you, make your cutoff rating even higher—probably double-A.

Avoid margining to the hilt. If your bonds fall in price, you may have to put up more money at a time when it is inconvenient. And bear in mind that it rarely pays to buy municipals on any margin at all. The interest on the loan will not be tax-deductible.

Finally, never forget the most important fundamental facts about bonds and the bond market. First, their chief and most common advantage is that they usually provide—or should provide—good income. Second, their chief and most common disadvantage is that they are not inflation-proof—or, to be more exact in this day of high interest rates, they are often only partially inflation-proof. Third, they should probably not be bought as a substitute for stocks. If you do buy them when the stock market is languishing, with the thought that you will later return to stocks, you should probably confine your choice to bonds with short maturities or to money market instruments such as U.S. Treasury bills. Fourth, never forget that bonds are bought and sold in a market dominated by and geared to large institutional investors.

This is changing somewhat. And it may change even more. But it is not likely to change so much that institutions still will not dominate the market and help govern everything that takes place in it.

All this reinforces the importance of weighing an investment in bonds just as carefully as you would weigh one in stocks or real estate or anything else. As they say, investigate before you invest.

Index

Catal

If you
book
and i
reque

McG
1221
New

DEMCO